D1124573

THE LAST OF THE
BIG-TIME BOSSES

THE LAST OF THE BIG-TIME BOSSES

*The Life and Times of Carmine De Sapio
and the Rise and Fall of Tammany Hall*

WARREN MOSCOW

STEIN AND DAY/*Publishers*/New York

First published in the United States of America in 1971
Copyright © 1971 by Warren Moscow
Library of Congress Catalog Card No. 79-160351
All rights reserved
Published simultaneously in Canada by Saunders of Toronto Ltd.
Designed by David Miller
Stein and Day/Publishers/7 East 48 Street, New York, N.Y. 10017
ISBN 0-8128-1400-2

AUTHOR'S NOTE

The material for this book was accumulated, in the main, in the course of the thirty-seven years I spent on the political scene as a newspaper reporter and city official. Most of it has never before been presented in perspective and much of it has never been disclosed at all.

When it came to writing about the several situations of which I did not have personal knowledge, I turned to the political figures who had been intimately concerned. I am grateful to them for their unhesitating assistance. I do not identify these latter-day sources, first because they spoke freely with the assurance that they would not be quoted, and secondly because to identify a particular source in any one situation might lead to the inference that he was responsible for other material as well, which would be incorrect and unfair. The inferences and political interpretations are my own.

CONTENTS

THE LAST OF THE
BIG-TIME BOSSES

THE BOSS SYNDROME

Carmine Gerard De Sapio, the last man to be boss of the political instrument known as Tammany Hall, was possibly the most powerful political boss of recent times. He was certainly the most controversial in the minds of people in politics and the most mysterious to the public at large.

A decade after he fell from power in 1961 the political woods remain populated with men and women who regard De Sapio as the best political boss they have ever known or heard of. They remember him with affection and, given the opportunity, will recall some personal involvement with him that demonstrated his innate decency and consideration for others. On the other hand, there are those who could not accept him as either legitimate or respectable, no matter what he did personally; to them, he was tainted by underworld support and Tammany slime. There are, of course, others who did not know him at all but who distrusted him simply because he was the boss, and they see only evil in the boss concept.

Carmine De Sapio entered the arena of big-time politics in New York when the old political machines based on patronage and corruption were dying anachronisms all over the nation. The once fearsome Tammany machine in New York was no exception. After De Sapio had worked his way up through the Tammany ranks to become the boss, he dedicated himself to reversing the national trend, to restoring the Tammany machine to power so remodeled and modernized that it could run efficiently in the new political climate.

By dint of hard work, force of personality, brilliant maneuvers, sound tactics, and good guesses he succeeded, but only for a time. When he finally erred—a miscalculation arising from overconfidence in the progress he had made—it was as though he had never succeeded at all. His first failure resulted in utter failure. The Tammany Hall for which he had worked so tirelessly to produce a new and more favorable image while restoring its old-time power became so discredited and unimportant that it even dropped its historic and unhallowed name.

Long after De Sapio's reign as boss of the Tammany machine and of the statewide party organization had come to an end and he was on his way to becoming just a political legend, he was convicted by a federal court jury of having conspired to bribe a public official and share in the proceeds of selling influence. Yet when he was sentenced to two years in prison, no cheering erupted on the sidelines. Those who accepted the jury's verdict as just, and those who did not, shared the feeling that they had witnessed a tragedy.

Tammany was the best known of all of the political machines the two-party system had produced in America. From the moment De Sapio formally took over the leadership of Tammany Hall in 1949, his approach to the job fascinated those who were in a position to follow it closely and puzzled those looking in from the outside, because he set out to be different from every other political boss, of Tammany or anywhere else.

The public's concept of a Tammany boss had been etched by Thomas Nast, the nineteenth-century political caricaturist whose cartoons in *Harper's Weekly* during the 1860s and 1870s created the elephant, the donkey, and the tiger as the symbols respectively of the Republican Party, the Democratic Party, and Tammany Hall. Nast's particular target was William Marcy Tweed, the head of a loose aggregation of ward heelers and thieves who had taken over what had once been a patriotic society known as the Society of Tammany and used it as their political front to control the Democratic Party in the city and state of New York.

In just one fifteen-month period in which their operations were later exposed, Tweed and three close associates in high city office milked the city of New York of the incredible sum of $30 million.

In his cartoons, Nast pictured Tweed in stripes, which were both the stripes of the Tammany tiger and the stripes of the prison uniforms of the era, and dubbed him "Boss Tweed." Tweed had a respectable middle-class background, but he was basically a thug, a powerful 280-pounder with a paunch that lent itself readily to Nast's artistry. Convicted, he spent a comfortable year in jail under the best conditions that his still potent influence could arrange, bribed his way out, and escaped in the dead of night to refuge in Spain.

He was eventually identified on the basis of Nast's cartoons, which had circulation abroad. He was extradited and died in prison. Tweed had no real interest in his party or the politics of the day, only in loot and high living. The development of Tammany Hall from the confederation of thieves that was the Tweed Ring into a disciplined political machine was the work of his successor, known as "Honest John" Kelly.

The public's concept of a Tammany boss as primarily a thief was fostered anew by Richard Croker, who followed Kelly. Croker grew rich enough from politics to retire, temporarily, to spend his time running racing stables in his native Ireland. When the consolidation of the outlying suburbs—Brooklyn, Queens, and Richmond (Staten Island)—into the previously existing City of New York became a fact in 1898, Croker returned and reassumed control so that he could personally manage the distribution of the larger loot now involved. He set up court in the biggest hotel in Lakewood, New Jersey, then the most fashionable winter resort for affluent New Yorkers, and picked a properly acquiescent man—Judge Robert Van Wyck—to be the first mayor of the enlarged political principality. Croker wore diamonds and generally flaunted his affluence, even though he had no visible means of support. And he did not give a damn what anyone thought. Asked by the investigator for a legislative committee if it was not true that he spent his political career working for his own benefit, he snarled, "Sure. I'm working for my pocket all the time, the same as you."

Charles Francis Murphy, whose rule of Tammany from 1902 to 1924 was the only one that exceeded De Sapio's twelve-year reign, did achieve some degree of respectability, but most of it came after his death and was based on the comparison of Murphy with some of the men who followed him. Murphy fostered the political careers of Alfred E. Smith, the state's first four-time governor; of James J. Walker, who as mayor of New York was the beloved symbol of the Roaring Twenties; of the solid Robert F. Wagner, Sr., later to shine in the U.S. Senate. Murphy's son-in-law, James A. Foley, was the most respected surrogate judge in the nation. Much of their glory rubbed off later on Murphy's bossdom, when Murphy himself was dead.

Murphy gave Smith and Wagner in particular a free hand in social legislation, preceding the New Deal by two decades, and lent their programs Tammany support in the legislature. But Murphy was the strong, silent type of boss who thought the mechanics of politics were none of the public's business, and even when he worked for the public good he did so behind the scenes. He had no hesitation in holding up businessmen for his own profit, using the power of his bossdom as the weapon. For example, when the Pennsylvania Railroad wanted to build Pennsylvania Station at Seventh Avenue and 33rd Street, it needed street-closing permits from the old Tammany-controlled Board of Aldermen. It did not get the permits until it agreed to award the excavation contracts to a company in which Murphy had a financial interest. This was open knowledge at the time. When Murphy died he left an estate valued at $2 million, even though he had had no visible means of support during the period of his political leadership. In the more tolerant age in which Murphy lived, scandals involving a political boss caused only a ripple on the political waters. Many were surprised only at the moderation of Murphy's take.

From any point of view, Carmine De Sapio was different from each of his best-known predecessors. Unlike Tweed, he was never caught or even accused of tapping the city treasury. Unlike Croker, he lived unostentatiously and did give a damn what the people thought. He was as much aware as any of his critics of the mud that had spattered him as he moved through the miasmic Tammany swamp, and his concern with the new De Sapio version of Tammany was that it should look clean and stay clean.

Murphy never made a public speech, never talked to a reporter if he could avoid it, and shunned every aspect of publicity. De Sapio avidly sought publicity and exposure to the public. He saw himself as a political evangelist and laughed off the advice of friends to stay away from the spotlight. He lectured at Ivy League colleges, wrote for the press, and made speeches at public dinners, always preaching his gospel that political organization is vital and important to every citizen because politics is the motive power of government.

De Sapio's predecessors had entrenched themselves in control of their machines by means of job patronage. They put enough people to work in the various branches of government, and at all levels, so that when voting time came around the ballots of all the office-holders, including those down at the level of cleaners and clerks, and the ballots of all their sisters, cousins, and aunts were enough to give the machine a solid election base, almost in itself enough for victory. This type of patronage was no longer in existence when De Sapio's bossdom began, due to the spread of the civil service concept. So De Sapio aimed his appeal at the public at large. He maneuvered his Tammany organization, and later the Democratic Party as a whole, into being identified with the "right side" of public issues. He saw that as the only road open which guaranteed continuing success at the polls.

While other bosses had grabbed what they could when they could, De Sapio played the long-range game, even to the selection of his candidates for major public office. The governors, mayors, and borough presidents enthroned by Tweed and Croker and even Murphy in his early years were expected by them to be as corrupt as the bosses or complacent enough to look away. De Sapio never selected a candidate for major office whose political armor was tarnished or who lacked independence of mind. To those who thought they knew the boss syndrome, this was all very strange and confusing.

It was cartoonist Nast, lambasting Tweed, who gave the title "Boss" its place in the vocabulary of politics. The boss system itself, of which Tweed was only the most spectacular manifestation, was in itself a spontaneous outgrowth of the two-party system that became embedded in American politics in the 1860s and lasted without serious challenge for a century thereafter. ✓

The boss system sprouted and then flourished because a party had to remain alive from one election to the next, and for that it needed some kind of continuing machinery as well as mechanics willing to devote full time to keeping it well oiled and in good repair. The mechanics proved to be as available in politics as they always have been in fraternal groups, parent-teacher organizations, or nonpartisan associations of good citizens like the League of Women Voters. Those who stay around to do the work exercise the power. Thus political history from the latter days of the Civil War is studded with the names of men who began as spear carriers and wound up as bosses of the political armies.

Whether their activity was at the local, state, or national level, their constant attention to party affairs operated to give them control. They developed the art of reconciling factional differences, of keeping a majority satisfied. And since their party was willing to let them run things, they were able year in and year out to nominate for office the man who would serve them and their party's purpose while he functioned as alderman, state legislator, mayor, governor, U.S. senator or representative, or even, in one case, President of the United States.

Neither party had a monopoly of the boss system or of the corruption that was so often its handmaiden. In the history books the boss who overshadows even Tweed was a Republican and big businessman: Marcus Alonzo Hanna of Ohio. Hanna is the only boss on record who picked a man with the intention of grooming him for the presidency and got him into the White House. The *Columbia Encyclopedia* describes Hanna thus:

A characteristic American capitalist of the Gilded Age. He became a dealer in coal and iron mines, furnaces, lake shipping and shipbuilding, a bank, a newspaper, an opera house, and a street-railway system. He was active in politics and by 1890 was the ruling power in the Ohio Republican party. He was instrumental in having William McKinley elected governor of Ohio in 1891 and again in 1893. Hanna...groomed him for the presidency in 1895, and was responsible for his nomination by the Republicans in 1896. Hanna, as chairman of the Republican National Committee, boldly made that campaign a defense of business and property... and on that basis secured heavy financial contributions from "big business." ...Hanna was a great party leader who significantly exemplified the union between business and politics for the purposes of economic policy rather than for personal graft.

Hanna, with his own great wealth, could afford to think in terms of economic power rather than personal graft. But to put over his candidate, McKinley, he had to work with bosses from other states. And all over the country, the partnership between business and Republican politics at the state level was blatantly evil and corrupt, before, during, and after Hanna's time.

For the ordinary state boss the principal political prize was control of the state legislature, rather than the then-feeble federal establishment. In the burgeoning states of the West and the rapidly industrializing North—where the action and the money were—the Republicans usually held political control. With the electorate still voting "the way they had shot" in the Civil War, the GOP could wave the bloody shirt of the late rebellion and keep the Democrats in the minority.

To the extent that business was regulated at all, the legislatures controlled all of the regulatory fields, including those later taken over by Congress and federal agencies. A business could not get a certificate of incorporation without a special law passed for that purpose. The railroads, public utilities, and banks depended for their existence—and continued prosperity—on legislative whim. U.S. senators were elected by the majorities in each state legislature, not by the people of the state. A good part of the senator's Washington business was to fend off any federal incursion on states' rights, and to approve for the federal judiciary only those candidates whose view of the Constitution was that the document imposed little federal authority on business.

All these factors made stakes at the legislative level so important that big business felt impelled to deal with someone—i.e., a boss—who could deliver a legislative majority for whatever big business needed or wanted. When big business found its man, it supported him thereafter with whatever cash or favors the situation required.

17

In his autobiography William Allen White, the famed Kansas editor, recalls Cy Leland, an otherwise unsung boss of Kansas before the turn of the twentieth century. Leland's stock in trade consisted of the largesse of the railroads, which issued to him for distribution free passes to anywhere, at a time when the railroad represented the only form of land transportation other than man's two feet, the saddle-horse, or the buggy. The passes, good for one year on the donating railroad as well as on its theoretical competitors, went to legislators, newspaper reporters, and editors like White himself, and to the party members who participated in the local district caucuses where the nomination of legislators originated.

If the situation required it, railroad cash was always available, and distributed by Leland right down to the election-precinct level, to guarantee that the party's candidates would vote "right" on rail-road issues and accept without question the potential U.S. senator whom the railroad had privately chosen. Leland was only one boss operating within one state. His counterparts were everywhere. And if it was not the railroad which was buying legislators, it was some other big-business interest which happened to be paramount in the particu-lar state. References to the "coal senator" or the "steel senator" or the "bank senator" were commonplace and shocked no one.

The business/boss alliance was also good for a lot of votes on election day. Big business had a pervasive influence on local small businesses, particularly through the power of the local banker. The local businessman had a similar influence over his employees, not only because he exemplified success but because he could fire re-calcitrant employees or lock out his whole staff without worrying about trade unions or labor boards.

The boss set-up on the Democratic side differed in form, though not in ethical values or objectives. The successful Democratic ma-chines existed chiefly in the cities, but not all of them. Where they had been able to get control, their bosses were just as willing to sell water, gas, or trolley-car franchises directly to cash bidders as their Republican counterparts did more indirectly at the state level, but their basic clientele was the masses, rather than the middle class, whom the Republicans had preempted.

In the city ghettoes there were saloons, gambling houses, and prostitutes to be protected, for a price, from paying a penalty for violating laws. There were jobs on the public payroll to be parceled out, for the competitive civil service was not even born until 1884 and remained a weak and puling infant for decades thereafter. The city boss could reward a follower with a job—as policeman, garbage collector, street inspector, watchman, or office clerk—with tenure at the pleasure of the boss.

The boss system took the immigrant fresh off the boat and made him an American citizen. It found him a place to live, kissed his babies, entertained his whole family on the district club's annual boat ride, picnic, or clambake, which was the event of the year in a lower-class society of limited pleasures. It fixed traffic tickets and jury notices for the shopkeeper, winked at the building and sanitary-code violations by the landlord or sweatshop operator, reduced tax assessments for big property owners. The boss system made money for the boss and for the party organization, but it also made life more bearable for a lot of little people who had no access otherwise to government, who knew of its operations only through their contacts with the machine. Tammany and its counterparts were whipping boys for the editorial writers in their ivory towers, but they were friends to the man in the street.

Machines of opposite parties rarely battled more than once for control of the same constituency. Once a machine was in control, its rule tended to shrivel the opposition, whose membership gravitated to where the power was, thus entrenching the ins still deeper. This in turn made the control of the nominating process the major concern of the machine, since its nominee would be, barring unusual circumstances, the sure winner in the general election.

In the beginning of the two-party system, nominations were made at a caucus, to which everyone was invited to share in the naming of the men who would carry the party's banner in the election ahead. American political ingenuity being what it is, the caucus system soon became a tool for control of the nominating process by the boss. He made the arrangements for the caucus, and his lieutenants drummed up the kind of a crowd that would carry out whatever the boss had

19

already decided. If substantial opposition seemed likely, the boss would see that the date and hour of the meeting was disclosed only to his own followers, and the secret was kept until it was too late for the others to organize. Or he picked for his convention hall the back room of some waterfront saloon, where the opposition could be intimidated or persuaded by free booze.

Eventually the caucus system was hounded out of existence by political reformers, most of them from the western states, who demanded the setting up of a party-primary system. They thought that this would end boss domination and thus big-business control of their legislatures. In many parts of the nation, including New York, the bosses acted quite early to give the voters the form of a primary, but not its substance, to silence the clamor. The boss made the primary rules, kept permanent possession of party membership rolls, and furnished the ballots which the party members could use for voting. This enabled the machine to keep permanent "floaters" on the books —men who voted as often and as fast as their legs could carry them between the various polling places where they were registered under different names.

Another instrument for fraud was the "cannon" ballot, probably so named because a few cannons could blow the opposition sky-high. The cannon consisted of as many as a dozen paper ballots which had been marked in advance, folded together, and patiently compressed with an old-fashioned flatiron, so that the original wad was no thicker than a single ballot. A loyal organization family would spend hours at the ironing board. On primary day the cannon was dropped into the ballot box with the connivance of the election inspector, who palmed the surplus ballot stubs as he tore off the entire batch. When the time came to count the ballots, the box was shaken vigorously before it was opened, so that the separate sheets of the cannon were mixed before they were extracted.

In New York it took the primary-election system the full biblical three score years and ten to achieve equality of status with the general election. The process started in the 1890s and got its first big push forward in the first decade of the twentieth century when Governor Charles Evans Hughes was the local apostle of the national political-reform movement that marked the era of Theodore Roosevelt and Woodrow Wilson. Hughes pushed through the New York legislature a primary law which gave legal status to what had previously been unofficial, unsupervised primary operations, over the opposition of both Democratic and Republican bosses.

But even after the strides made under Hughes, the parties still printed their own ballots and counted their own votes. It was 1922 before the primary came completely under the general-election law, and it was the middle 1960s before the fraud-proof voting machine replaced the paper ballot in primary elections. And every step of the way the bosses and their machines managed to accommodate themselves to the reform-sponsored primary system. In acting to minimize the political effect of primary reform, the major parties acted as a team. In the legislature their representatives who wrote the election law made the provisions so technical—in the guise of protection against fraud—that newcomers attempting to qualify for a primary fight were constantly in trouble. The bipartisan machinery set up to run elections, known as the Board of Elections, operated under just one theme during the period when primary petitions were submitted to the board for acceptance or rejection. It was "Down with the insurgents."

So despite the hopes that the reformers had for it, the primary system never succeeded in haltering the boss system in New York. Long after the primary had become part of the election machinery, the party machine retained the edge. Its people could be counted on to come out and vote, and the machine had the know-how. A rough rule of thumb was that the organization could not be beaten in a primary election unless (1) the opposition to it included a segment of the organization itself, which would furnish experienced manpower at the polls, and (2) there was a moral issue, or the appearance of one, which could be developed to bring out the general public.

What did sound the death knell for the boss system in New York was the decline of the political machine itself for reasons both within and beyond its own control. And New York was the bellwether for the nation. Just as it had originally led in creating the political machine, so did it set the pace for its discard. But the process was long and slow.

The first to be stricken was the Republican state machine, which took a full thirty years a-dying. At the turn of the century its undisputed boss was Thomas C. Platt, who ran a more than usually corrupt legislature with an iron hand for the benefit of himself and his big-business allies. He also used it to secure the election of both himself and Chauncey M. Depew as U.S. senators. Depew, famous for decades as America's greatest after-dinner speaker, was a "railroad senator" who openly acted as counsel to the New York Central Railroad and sat on its board of directors while serving in Congress.

Hughes, a devotedly honest Republican political activist, made Platt and Depew particular targets of investigations. Acting as counsel for an investigation brought about by public pressure, Hughes pried first into legislative corruption. He showed Depew to have been secretly on the payroll of a large insurance company which was under fire for mulcting its policyholders. When these and other headlines made Hughes governor, he ripped apart the boss system in his own party. Depew retired to private life. Platt died just as Hughes was leaving the governorship for the United States Supreme Court.

Under the subsequent leadership of William Barnes and later the combined direction of Charles D. Hilles and H. Edmund Machold, the New York GOP maintained close but not as obviously corrupt ties with big business. Hilles, one-time secretary to William Howard Taft and director of Taft's hopeless bid for reelection as President in 1912, was the state's national committeeman from 1912 to 1936. Machold alternated as speaker of the state assembly, Republican state chairman, and back-bench boss during most of the same period. Hilles was the courtly representative of the New York party in matters of national politics and interstate big-business interests; Machold's alliance was primarily with the public utility companies that generously financed the GOP at the state level, even though it no longer had U.S. senatorships for sale. The Seventeenth Amendment to the Constitution, effective in 1913, took the power to elect U.S. senators away from the legislature and gave it to the electorate.

The Hilles-Machold ties with business were generally more

respectable and conservative than those of their predecessors, but their rule of the party placed it on the unpopular side of issues of the day, such as social reform and national prohibition. Finally, the collapse of big business during the Great Depression of the 1930s removed it temporarily as a political force, and Hilles retired from politics. Machold also quit during the depression, when an airing of his party's alliances with the gas, electric, and telephone companies showed that the utilities still exerted a corrupting influence on legislative policies.

From the mid-1930s to the present, the Republication Party in the state never had a boss worthy of the title except for two men who were publicly identified in another capacity. They were Thomas E. Dewey and Nelson Rockefeller, who used the power of their office —the governorship—and in Rockefeller's case his personal fortune as well, to dominate what was left of the party machine.

Dewey and Rockefeller, who were recognized by the public as officeholders rather than bosses, serve to point up a similar trend elsewhere. In Chicago, first Mayor Ed Kelly and later Mayor Richard Daley drew their political power, and hence their political longevity, from public rather than party office. So did the Byrd family in Virginia.

In New York the decline of the Republican machine served at first to make the Democratic boss system seem more entrenched than ever before. But the Democratic boss system also was to take its beating, from a series of blows which it did not feel or even comprehend at the time they were originally dealt.

A time bomb was planted under Tammany Hall as early as 1921, when the machine seemed at the height of its power and prestige. Charles F. Murphy, its leader, was even thinking of the possibility of nominating and electing a President of the United States. His candidate was the great Al Smith. But while the Smith boom was still a glint in Murphy's eye, Congress passed the first immigration restriction law. By setting up a quota system, the law cut to a trickle the stream of indigent immigrants from southern and eastern Europe.

New York's Ellis Island had become world-famous as the first port of call for the millions seeking a new life in America. A high percentage stayed in the city where they landed, and they helped build it into the world's greatest. But when they first stepped off the crowded immigrant ships, they needed help, the day-by-day assistance and attention that Tammany had geared itself to give. Tammany needed these twentieth-century immigrants as replacements for those who had arrived earlier and whose children were now emerging from the slums. The second and third generations of immigrant families had gotten schooling their parents or grandparents lacked. With their knowledge of English and ready adaptability for jobs, their ties to the political machine were based less on necessity than on convenience.

The Tammany machine had been accustomed to turning immigrants into voting citizens so fast their heads whirled, and then drawing on them for years thereafter for political support. The district political clubs stayed open evenings to keep warm and constant the relationship with the ghetto clientele. The leader himself was on hand to consider every request for help and arrange for its fulfillment. If legal advice was needed, the friendly clubhouse lawyer, being groomed for a future judgeship, handed it out without fee. The boss's lieutenant always had a buck or two to pay the supplicant's back milk bill. The leader's card, with an introductory scrawl, was good for a job at a local business establishment or factory whose owner owed the leader a favor.

When the source of new material for proselytizing—immigration—was cut off, the effects were not immediately apparent. Tammany prospered as never before during the 1920s from the newly illegal liquor trade, its district clubhouses operated at full blast, and no one thought twice that the faces at the club every night were old and familiar. The absence of replacement fodder for Tammany's army went unnoticed until Tammany faced losing election battles and found it had no reinforcements for its dwindling cadres.

Chronologically speaking, the next major blow at Tammany was dealt by the Seabury investigation. This was actually three separate probes into Tammany wrongdoing, running consecutively in 1930, 1931, and 1932. Samuel Seabury, descended from a long line of Protestant bishops, and himself a former judge of the state Court

24

of Appeals and one-time ally of William Randolph Hearst when the publisher was an anti-Tammany crusader, aired Tammany's operations from top to bottom and exposed the organization as corrupt beyond imagination.

Seabury's first investigation, carried on as an agent of the state's court hierarchy, dealt with the buying of places on the Criminal Court bench, then called Magistrate's Court, and the fixes in that court which were made for those who could pay for their liberty. In the second inquiry, as agent of Governor Franklin Delano Roosevelt, Seabury reported on the inside workings of the office of the district attorney of New York County, which did not seem able to convict many major criminals. Seabury showed that the district attorney, a pillar of both Tammany Hall and Trinity Church, was a senile septuagenarian who did not think clearly after the first two hours in his office each day, time his assistants spent wearing him out by submitting routine matters. The assistants spent the rest of the day not in prosecuting criminals, but in getting the weary old man to sign, uncomprehendingly, papers dismissing cases against the politically well-connected.

The public furor resulting from the first two probes led to full-scale investigation of the entire city government, with Seabury this time as both counsel for and field marshal of a special committee created by the Republican-controlled state legislature, with the broadest possible powers of subpoena. Seabury proved to be a genius in tracing the course and final resting place of bribe monies. The dragnets he devised to uncover secret bank accounts and safe-deposit boxes became standard tools for later investigations in many scattered fields.

Seabury concentrated his heaviest fire on Tammany, which had always been the senior among the five separate Democratic county organizations in the city. When Murphy's leadership of Tammany got under way in 1902 the city consolidation was only four years old, and Tammany ruled at the seat of power and wealth. Later Murphy directed the carving out of the Bronx as a separate county, instead of just the northern reaches of New York. He set up the Bronx as a separate political machine, but always hand-picked its leader and controlled its actions. Relations with the Queens and Brooklyn organizations were less firm, but no one challenged Murphy's city-wide leadership and Tammany's right to the largest share of the spoils.

Mayor Jimmy Walker, taking office a year after Murphy's death, privately enhanced his own power by dealing in patronage directly with each county leader, rather than passing it all through Tammany Hall for distribution. However, for the sake of appearances, he supported the fiction that John F. Curry, the man Walker had put in as Tammany leader, was the boss of the entire city.

Since Tammany had enjoyed the most power, it had got the most graft, and thus Tammany's insiders were the prime targets for exposure by Seabury, who hammered away seeking the real sources of the income their bank records disclosed. For example, New York sheriff Tom Farley, a Tammany district leader, had accumulated hundreds of thousands of dollars beyond the total of his salary over the years. His explanation, extracted from him by Seabury bit by bit as he squirmed in the witness chair, has passed into the American language, part of the folklore of politics. He swore that whenever he needed money, he went to "a little tin box" he had in his home, and took it from there.

Deputy City Clerk James J. McCormick, another Tammany district leader, who presided over the thousands of City Hall marriages in his office in the Municipal Building, was exposed as a cheap bully who kept his desk drawer open so that the bridegroom, afraid of looking cheap and losing caste on his wedding day, would drop a ten- or twenty-dollar bill into the drawer as a tip.

Even the brilliantly witty, altogether charming and delightful Mayor Walker wound up looking sheepish and harassed after hours of trying to convince the dogged Seabury, and the public, where his money had come from. It was known to Walker's intimates that Seabury had traced only part of it, but even the visible cash was large in total and unexplained as to source.

Governor Roosevelt removed the beetle-browed, hulking Farley, laying down for the first time the rule that a man holding public office owed the people a reasonable explanation of his sources of income. While ostensibly Farley was the target of this dictum, it was an arrow aimed at Walker as well. The mayor resigned, voicing a protest against the unfairness of the charges filed against him. He did so just one step ahead of his removal from the mayoralty by the governor.

The Seabury revelations coincided with the worst of the depression years. In New York one man out of four was jobless, and most of the rest worked at reduced wages. Private charities had exhausted their funds, and the public welfare system had yet to be born. Graft was not amusing to a man with an empty stomach. The voters put into perspective the favors the district leader had done for them and the hundreds of thousands of dollars he was shown to have stashed away. The businessman and shopkeeper whose profits were nonexistent stopped contributing cash or goods to "them crooks"—the same men he had welcomed as "fixers" in more prosperous times. The result of all this was the election in 1933 of Fiorello H. La Guardia as the city's first reform mayor since John Purroy Mitchel in 1913, and the loss by Tammany of control of every city department, including the police.

Tammany had resented Franklin Roosevelt's cooperation with the Seabury probes, although the reformers felt he had moved more slowly than he should have, and eventually only because his hand had been forced. But the worst for Tammany was still to come. The damage that Roosevelt as governor did to Tammany was petty compared with the devastating effect his policies as President had on the Tammany machine and its counterparts everywhere in the nation.

Again, this was not immediately apparent. In Roosevelt's four successive elections to the presidency—1932, 1936, 1940, and 1944 —Tammany and the other Democratic political machines in the nation rode to victory on his coattails, electing governors, mayors, U.S. senators and representatives who otherwise would have stood no chance. The machines began to look upon Roosevelt as heavensent. How could one lose a local election if one yelled loudly enough in praise of FDR? In addition, the patronage in the form of public-works contracts and federal jobs flowed from the newly centralized government in Washington as never before.

The men running the machines did not see—and could not have

done anything about it if they had—that Roosevelt's New Deal was the most formidable enemy the machine system had ever known. Roosevelt's job-creating agencies, the Works Projects Administration, Public Works Administration, Civil Conservation Corps, and his social security and unemployment-insurance programs, were competition as disastrous for the machine's own welfare state as Macy's was to the old corner dry-goods store. The voter was now able to get from government as a matter of right what he previously had received from the machine. If he needed or just wanted more, he could stand up and yell for it as a free and independent citizen, and not fear the disfavor of a boss or charges of ingratitude. This impact of the welfare state on the Tammany system first became apparent in the latter 1940s, and the author gave it recognition in a *Saturday Evening Post* article in April 1947, in a piece entitled "Political Machines Have Lost Their Grip."

In those same years, from 1937 through 1946, another Roosevelt invention, the labor union with the power of the federal government behind it, struck the machines still another blow. The machines had once been the only apparatus equipped to do election canvassing, to dragoon the voters to the polls. By the 1940s the immigration curb of two decades before had pared the machine manpower, and now the trade and industrial unions were feeling their oats. The union shop stewards had plenty of political experience gained in internal conflict. Once they turned their hand to public elections, they became a force to be reckoned with by the political machines. In Chicago, for example, Mayor Ed Kelly called upon labor unions as early as the presidential election of 1940 to participate in the preelection canvassing and supplement his own waning manpower at the polling places. In Detroit the automobile workers became the most potent political force in the city, and even in the whole state of Michigan.

In New York President Roosevelt had encouraged the garment-trades unions to organize politically by creating the American Labor Party, to aid his own reelection campaign in 1936. The following year the ALP swung into line as a supporter of La Guardia for reelection as mayor, and its threat was alarming enough to force the local Republicans to back the Little Flower for a second term, though their leadership resented his independence. The ALP furnished La Guardia's majority in that second election—1937—and it so served him for a third term four years later.

The final blow to Tammany was not planned by anybody: it was the size of the vote attracted to the polls in the Roosevelt years that spelled the end. Before the Roosevelt era the number of Americans who voted regularly was relatively small. The Roosevelt policies excited the public, aroused controversy, and brought home to the working man the intimate connection between the actions of the government in Washington and the contents of the family pocketbook at home. Since it is a political axiom that "people vote their pocketbooks," Roosevelt was the principal beneficiary, but the turnout also established a new voting pattern, one of participation. More people came to the polls in the Roosevelt era than ever before, and long after Roosevelt died they continued to vote en masse. They had got into the habit and it stuck with them, even at the local election level.

Consider the pre-Roosevelt mayoralty election of 1929 in New York City. The opponents were Jimmy Walker, running for a second term; La Guardia, a candidate for the first time, and shocking even some of his own supporters among the Republicans by his seemingly wild (but later proven) charges against Tammany; and Norman Thomas, the socialist, who was getting considerable support from conservative upper-class groups who could not stand La Guardia's radicalism. The vote cast in this more than usually lively contest was 1,409,000 in a city with a population numbering 6,840,000.

Twenty years later, in a very similar political atmosphere, with William O'Dwyer seeking a second term in City Hall, the total vote divided by three candidates was 2,578,000, out of a population of 7,835,000. Thus it can be seen that in actual count the number of people voting went up more than the city's population, reflecting a much higher degree of political interest.

That kind of vote increase meant that the machines could no longer control the election process. In the heyday of their power Tammany and its allies in the other boroughs controlled about

700,000 bedrock votes—votes that would be cast under the Democratic emblem even for a yellow dog, as they sometimes were. The Republicans could count on a similarly loyal 300,000. In a total vote like that of 1929 the Tammany candidate's guarantee of election was solid. But when the vote went up to 2,500,000 and higher, Tammany's 700,000 could only affect the election result, not determine it.

Of all the factors that figured in the decline of Tammany Hall—the shutting off of immigration; Seabury; the Roosevelt welfare state; the rise of the labor unions; the increased vote—only one was immediately obvious to the ward politicians who suffered through the politically bleak 1930s and 1940s. This was the Seabury investigations, with the scarlet stain of scandal attached to Tammany thereby. The Tammany politicians felt that if they could just get that monkey off their backs, if they could just win an election with a man of their own, happy days would be here again. So they called for new leadership that would produce such a result; they changed leaders the way a seventh-place baseball club fires managers; they even clung to the Roosevelt they once had scorned. They tried every device but genuine reform. And as they waited for someone somehow to rescue them, their machine became weaker and weaker and sank lower and lower.

It was left to Carmine De Sapio to start Tammany on its comeback trail.

TWO

CLIMBING THE LADDER

In the broad scope of the political spectrum most of the men and women the public identifies as politicians devote much more time and effort to the party or public office they hold than do the average men and women engaged in private enterprise. They work as hard as they do for a variety of motives: the power and the glory that may come their way; the itch to figure in government annals or history books; the need to seem important to family and friends; belief in some specific cause or program; or for the money that can be made out of politics.

The normal politician, despite his work load, still manages to carry on a private life of some kind—he sneaks in a quick vacation, an evening at the theater or a hockey game, time with his wife and children at home or with friends. He has even been known to talk of things other than politics when he is given the chance. But there is also another breed of politician, small in number and recognized even by other politicians as something special. These men are more than politicians, they are "political animals." The term is not derogatory. It means that the person so identified has demonstrated that politics is his sole interest in life. He doesn't even know there is an alternative to letting politics interrupt his breakfast or force him to nibble at five public dinners in one evening. For him there are no Sundays or holidays or other days away from the job, because there is always some political chore—which he does not regard as such— that requires his time and attention. He may love his wife, but he takes it as a matter of course that she understands politics comes first.

The difference between the politician and the political animal is that the politician is aware of the time he spends at his job and sometimes resents it, and the political animal is unaware of it and would be amazed at the suggestion that he might resent the requirements of his career. Lyndon Johnson and Richard Nixon showed themselves as political animals early in their careers. So did Carmine De Sapio.

What made them so? There is no explanation but that they were born that way. As for motivation, De Sapio had one additional stimulus, the desire to show that an Italian could make good in a field up to then dominated by the Irish, and this in turn stemmed from the political conditions of the area in which he was born and in which he grew up.

The first time the name Carmine De Sapio got any attention from New York newspapers was on September 20, 1939, in the reporting of the primary election held the day before. The really big news that morning concerned World War II, which was still in its opening month. Streamer headlines across the front pages told the story that Adolf Hitler, fresh from his slaughter of the Polish army and populace, was launching a propaganda peace offensive to convince the world that his basic intentions were friendly. The story of the primary election was tucked in a corner of the first page of *The New York Times*. It owed even that degree of prominence to tradition rather than competitive news value, since the major contest had been for the Democratic nomination for a place on the Criminal Court bench in Manhattan.

The story continued to an inside page far back in the paper, where there was a secondary political story reporting the contests for Democratic and Republican party positions. It told of a riot call received at the Charles Street police station in Greenwich Village at 11 P.M., after the polls had closed. The call had emanated from P.S. 3, at Hudson and Grove Streets, a still respectably maintained old school that sheltered the polling booths for the 37th Election District of the First Assembly District West. The neighborhood was a middle-class section of the Village, housing mostly people who had been born there, plus a more recent scattering of artists and writers and their camp followers.

It took twenty policemen to restore order. When they did, they learned that the pro-establishment chairman of the district election board had been trying to steal the election and had been caught in the act. This had provoked the intended victims, and harsh words were followed by flying fists. The guilty operator had concealed a tiny pencil in his palm at the base of his fingers. As he handled the paper ballots, theoretically for a first count to see how many had been taken from the ballot boxes and how that count compared with the number of signatures in the registry book, he used the stub to make second markings on ballots that had been cast for the insurgents, thus invalidating them.

The trick was old and familiar to most professional poll workers. This particular election chairman was definitely a pro, working without the slightest sentimental involvement. In the first place, he was a Republican and the fight he was fixing was between two Democrats. Also, he did not even live in the district but had been imported from East Harlem, which could not have happened without hanky-panky at the central office of the city Board of Elections. He did get a small fee for services as a member of the election board, but his major political connection was that he was a deputy sheriff of New York County, and at the polls that evening he was working in the best interests of his superior in that job.

The establishment was represented in the primary contest by Daniel E. Finn, Jr., sheriff of New York County. The shrievalty then was a political sinecure involving no law-enforcement duties, just supervision of the serving of civil writs, and even there on a small scale. But the office was heavily manned by small-time politicians who were paid but did not work. Finn had been nominated for this plum by virtue of his standing as a district leader of Tammany Hall and elected to it as a result of the tendency of Manhattan voters to support anyone who ran for anything as a Democrat, unless they had been alerted to substantial grounds for opposition. Finn's Tammany district was the First Assembly District West.

Finn's father had been sheriff and district leader before him. So had his grandfather, the original Dan Finn in Tammany politics, famous at the turn of the century as "Battery Dan." In this 1939 primary the Finn district leadership was at stake.

The intended victim of the fraud attempted by the supporters of

Finn was Carmine De Sapio. Carmine was thirty-one, and in seeking Finn's district leadership was making his first serious bid for a major political post. Up to two years before, he had been Finn's principal lieutenant in running the political affairs of the district.

A word about the district, which included then all of what was the picturesque and unique Village as well as considerable other territory. It was a political fiefdom that once had been heavily populated. Its five-story tenements had housed the more recent Irish and Italian immigrants, and the three-story brownstones and town houses were occupied by those who had arrived earlier and worked their way up to middle-class comforts. By 1939 a lot of the original dwellings to the south and west had been demolished and that territory had become heavily industrialized.

Factory and loft buildings, the Holland Tunnel plazas, government office buildings, newspaper plants, and telephone-company skyscrapers took up the old space, but housed no voters. The construction of the Seventh and Eighth Avenue subways had been accompanied by street widenings, which cut broad swaths through the old street patterns and eliminated many residences. On the political maps the district still ran from 14th Street south to the Battery, and from Broadway west to the Hudson River, but the voting strength that remained was concentrated in the Village and in the area known as Little Italy directly to the south. In the Democratic primary the Italian vote was negligible, since most of the Italians then were Republicans, if they were enrolled in any party at all. It was the Irish vote in the Village that swung political control.

Finn and De Sapio were battling for the district leadership within a framework invented by Tammany Hall for its own purposes. The district leadership carried with it the power to dictate local nominations for public office; to hand out public jobs to the party faithful; to dicker with other district leaders over nominations which crossed district lines, such as those for the state senate and Congress; and to sit as a member of the executive committee of Tammany Hall.

But the job, and its perquisites, existed completely outside the provisions of the statewide election law that supposedly governed intraparty as well as interparty affairs. Under the Tammany system the district leader was picked as local boss by a show of hands of the legally elected members of the county committee from the area, and as they raised their hands they transferred to their leader the decision-making power the law said was theirs. Later on, when that district leader took his seat as a member of the executive committee of Tammany Hall, he cast his own vote for leader of Tammany Hall in an extralegal senate of party elders.

By show of hands or roll call in the committee session, the executive committee delegated to one of its own members the full executive political power of the Democratic Party of New York County. Until that selected member was deposed, resigned, or died, he was leader of Tammany Hall, the boss. And so it had been since the 1880s and the days of "Honest John" Kelly. Nowhere outside of Manhattan, except in the Bronx, which was historically Tammany's political descendant, did the right to boss a party rest in the hands of someone who had no official position under the election law.

County committee members everywhere in both major parties were elected on a ratio of committeemen to enrolled voters. This was set by party rule rather than by the election law. So Tammany, to ensure that the real political power stayed at the top, used a ratio that could result in as many as 17,000 county committeemen from the 994 election districts on Manhattan Island. Its version of participatory democracy had been designed to guarantee that the county committee would be so large that it could not function as a deliberative body. The system also had the advantage for the machine of giving it a tremendous number of trained political cadres, proud of their status as committeemen, to canvass for votes before general elections and to protect the "ins" in a contested primary.

Under the system as it existed, neither Dan Finn's nor Carmine De Sapio's name appeared on the primary ballot as candidate for district leader. Instead, there were individual sets of ballots for each election district within the assembly district. These ballots carried in separate columns the slates of candidates for election to the county committee—possibly ten but up to twenty—with the number based on the ratio to the party vote the previous time around. Each slate consisted of people living in that election district who if elected to the county committee were pledged informally to vote for either De Sapio or Finn. Their stand for their candidate was disclosed to the voters by word of mouth or through campaign literature during the pre-primary campaign. At the polls it was permissible but pointless for the voter to split his ballot, so no one did. It was a winner-take-all slate in each election district.

For weeks before the primary, workers for both sides canvassed the enrolled Democrats in the First Assembly District West. Not for them was the modern pollster's method of interviewing a handful of representative voters and then reporting the trend. These workers climbed stairs from basement to fifth story in every tenement and talked to every voter they could find. And they knew where they all lived. Their work was to influence the voter, not merely count him one way or another. The task took training, strong legs, and personal identification with the people. The reward lay in winding up on the winning side.

In this particular Finn-De Sapio fight the canvassing convinced both sides that the sure districts for one side or another were so evenly matched in county-committee membership that the primary's result would be determined by who carried the Grove Street sector. That is why the Finn management imported the outside professional to deface the De Sapio ballots cast there; that is why De Sapio himself was at the Grove Street school instead of at his headquarters, to make sure that the Finn crowd did not get away with larceny.

The district leadership for which Finn and De Sapio competed was by no means as prestigious or profitable as it would have been a decade earlier, for a large number of reasons.

In the ten years that followed 1929, short-sighted and blundering Tammany leadership at the top had led the machine into public conflict with both Franklin D. Roosevelt and Herbert H. Lehman. As President and governor respectively, they were the most powerful vote getters the state had ever known. Tammany's opposition helped rather than hurt them, and Tammany, as a result, looked silly if not stupid. Even when changes in the top leadership brought Tammany more nearly into line with the times, the machine still acted like the sulky elder child in the political family. It resented and seldom worked closely with the 100 percent pro-New Deal organizations in

Brooklyn and the Bronx and showed in petty ways its irritation at no longer being the cock of the political walk. And the more it sulked, the more it suffered from a falling off of federal and state patronage.

The door to City Hall was closed. Fiorello H. La Guardia had been mayor for six years. The Little Flower was independent of any brand of politics but his own. He was perfectly capable of dealing with Tammany district leaders if it suited his purpose—and it often did—but for campaign purposes and most of the year as well, Tammany was his pet target.

In New York County itself the district attorney was Thomas E. Dewey, the first of the "racket busters," who also made Tammany his particular target in the course of channeling his anticrime crusade into a boomlet for the Presidency of the United States. Tammany in 1939 was less concerned with Dewey's presidential prospects than with the fact that it could no longer staff the DA's office with its own clubhouse lawyers or put in "the fix" for its friends.

On top of all these tangibles, Tammany had lost caste with the public because the Seabury investigations had so firmly implanted the belief that the existing Tammany Hall was just the same old boodlebund it had been in the days of Tweed. In the intervening years Tammany had posed as Robin Hood. Its hypocrisy in that role was so thoroughly exploded that it was laughed at in an Inner Circle show (a New York City version of the Washington Gridiron dinner), written and produced by previously friendly and tolerant newspaper reporters. Parodying a popular song of the day, "Betty Coed," the reporters sang:

> Tammany Hall's a patriotic outfit,
> Tammany Hall's an old society.
> Fourth of July it always waves the flag, boys,
> But never will it waive immunity.

> Tammany Hall like Robin Hood professes
> To take things from the rich to give the poor
> But Tammany Hall gets just a bit confused sometimes
> And takes from both to give to Tammany Hall.

37

Many of the established and previously powerful leaders in Tammany had gone to jail or into retirement and oblivion. The ability of their successors to deliver traditional favors and protection from the law had dwindled. More and more contests for district leaderships were between Moe Tweedledee and Joe Tweedledum, with little at stake. Their partisans were either the outs trying to replace the ins in the hope that they could bring things back to normal or the ins trying desperately to maintain the status quo until somehow the good old days came back.

To outsiders the De Sapio-Finn affair looked like more of the same. But to the politically conscious of the Village, it was a deep-seated conflict that aroused strong emotions.

Sheriff Finn, usually referred to as "young Dan," was a short, slender, dapper man with a carefree manner, even when the situation seemed to call for a serious approach. He aroused little affection. His district captains had grumbled for years over how long it took them to find him to hand him a "contract," the vernacular for a requested political favor which required the approval of the leader. Many felt that things would be better if he spent more time at the Huron Club—the ancient political fortress of the Finns on Van Dam Street—and less in Village nightclubs and cafés. But he was a Finn, and his ousting would mean the end of an era, one more step away from the days when Tammany Hall was proud and powerful and the First Assembly District one of its major strongholds.

For the Irish in the Village as elsewhere, Tammany was the instrument which had enabled them to rise above oppression and derision, which had been their lot when they first appeared in America, and become the lords of politics. The installation of a new boss would also mean new lieutenants close to him, new jostling for position among the district's political elite.

So the Huron Club, or what was left of it, had its back to the wall, fighting for itself if not for young Dan. The De Sapio candidacy was in one important sense against all tradition. Italians had sought district leaderships before, but never against an Irishman and an Irish clan tradition, in predominantly Irish territory. To counteract this, De Sapio had ties based on admiration and affection, which

38

Finn did not, and there were few to contend that De Sapio had not earned respect. He had worked for that kind of hold on his neighbors long before he was old enough to vote.

He was born in the district on December 10, 1908, in a house at Varick and Grand Streets demolished a decade later for the street widening that accompanied the building of the Seventh Avenue subway. His father, Gerard, and mother, Marinetta, were Sicilian immigrants who had prospered moderately here. Gerard De Sapio owned a fleet of horse-drawn drays and ran his trucking business from an adjacent shed. A broad-shouldered, barrel-chested man, he was well known in the Village and was addressed as "Sheriff," because he had once been appointed an honorary deputy sheriff by the previous Sheriff Finn. Carmine was the first of two children, both sons. By the time he was ready for school, his parents could afford to send him to St. Alphonsus parochial school. Later he went to Fordham Prep and then to Fordham University, where he spent two years preparing to study law.

Carmine De Sapio never excelled as a student, but to his neighbors as well as his parents he was the model son, handsome, courteous, and responsible. What time he had free from school and dates with various girls in the neighborhood, who regarded him as very attractive, he spent doing political chores: his identification as a political animal was already beginning.

The Huron Club became his home away from home. He started running errands there while he was still in his teens. He was there to tote the bucket of coal up the tenement stairs to the needy family —of four, five, or six voters—whose kitchen coal stove was all that kept them from freezing in midwinter. In summer he lugged cakes of ice for those who could not afford the iceman. At Thanksgiving and Christmas the club gave out big holiday baskets filled with turkey and all the fixin's—the traditional holiday largesse of a political club—and they had to be delivered individually. Carmine lugged more than did most of the club's runners—his title in the hierarchy. In the late evening there might be the need for a fleet messenger to carry word to the desk sergeant at the Charles Street station to hold off booking one of "the boys" until more formal representations could be made in his behalf. All these errands and many more Carmine ran as a labor of love, with politics the object of his adoration.

It was thus not surprising that De Sapio decided quite early that politics was the career for him and that law—if he went through with his legal education—would be only a tool to aid his advancement. And even as he ran his errands he developed an approach which was to be a valuable political asset. It consisted of a special technique— the delivery of a favor.

Tammany in its Robin Hood role operated on the "You scratch my back and I'll scratch yours" philosophy. It did favors for people, and the people would return the favors by supporting the machine's candidates at the polls, thus keeping it in power and enabling it to continue doing favors. De Sapio was instinctively aware that no matter how warm were the thanks when a favor was bestowed, the gratitude was likely to wear thin with the passing of time. He sensed that people preferred being donors rather than recipients, that giving them a chance to feel it was they who had conferred the favor tied them to the machine even more closely and permanently.

So when he delivered the bucket of coal or cake of ice, he implied that the recipients were doing him a favor by taking it off his hands. If he shepherded unruly six-year-olds aboard an excursion boat or at the Huron Club's annual clambake, he managed to communicate to the mothers his gratitude for the chance to spend some time with their kids. As he listened to some hackneyed tale of family woe, he seemed to be a young man anxious to learn about life. The women of the district were particularly impressed that so handsome and active a young man was also so sympathetic. He got along well with women all his life, so much so that when he came up for trial at the end of his career, his attorney concentrated on getting women on the jury, undoubtedly in the hope that the magic would still be there.

In all his years as the boss of city and state politics, De Sapio used the techniques he had developed in the early Village years. He would call a man he knew to be eager for office and who filled the particular political bill of the moment and would ask modestly if he could "have the privilege" of presenting the man's name to the appropriate nominating group or appointing officer. His courtliness of manner earned him the title "the bishop" from the rough and tough members of the Tammany executive committee and inspired columnist Murray Kempton to dub him "the Norman Vincent Peale of politics." His choice of language was always on the side of understatement. To express complete agreement with a program of action being urged on him, his answer would be phrased, "I can see no reason why that should not be done." Or if asked for political intervention, his commitment would be, "I'll see what I can do."

All these mannerisms were his when he was still running errands on his native Village heath. In a locale where the dominant Irish tended to look down on the more recent immigrants clustered in Little Italy, De Sapio was both an exception and a revelation. His height, six feet, one inch, his broad shoulders, narrow waist, and long legs made him stand out physically, and his manners left no room for Irish ridicule.

He did have one physical handicap, his eyes. In his late teens he developed iritis, a rheumatism of the eyes which made study or extensive reading impossible (not that he had shown any extravagant tendencies in that direction). The ailment did kill off any possibility that he would go through with his law studies; it kept him away from the movies and the theater, and disqualified him for service in the armed forces in World War II. It hospitalized him frequently and mandated the constant wearing of dark-tinted glasses, later to become his political trademark.

Even when new medical knowledge made his hospital stays less frequent and of shorter duration, he still had to wear the dark glasses which gave him the appearance of a man of mystery even when his operations were in the open. The aura did not help when he later strove to create the "new image" of enlightened political leadership. But it did reinforce his decision to stick to politics as a career: he could still deal with people—read them, not books—and be a success.

His parents cooperated fully and sympathetically. They made it possible for him to work at politics full time, if necessary without salary or the prospect of financial reward. "Sheriff" De Sapio had already sold his draying business to the United States Trucking Company and invested the proceeds in a bungalow colony in the

Rockaways. The De Sapios were absentee landlords, and when the time came young Carmine went on the family payroll as manager of the colony, at $70 a week, with only nominal duties.

The De Sapios stayed in the Village as Carmine moved steadily up in the hierarchy of the Huron Club, from runner to assistant election-district captain, to captain and then to first lieutenant to Finn. His first job on the public payroll, a recognition of his standing in the club, came when he was twenty-nine. He was appointed secretary to a City Court judge at $3,000 a year. The then City Court was a civil court of limited jurisdiction, and the secretary to a City Court judge did not have to be learned in the law or even know how to type or take dictation. It was purely a patronage sinecure that gave its holder a desk and a telephone along with the salary—which in those days was free of federal income taxes—and a title that marked him as an organization man on the way up.

That same year, 1937, De Sapio married the charming Terese Natale, a New Jersey belle with friends in the Village, whom he met at a Saturday-night church dance. The young couple set up housekeeping in a six-room apartment on Charlton Street, where the rent was $55 a month. What more could a young man want?

For the politically dedicated De Sapio, the answer was easy. He. wanted the district leadership. The split with Finn that this involved was not hard to justify. Finn was goofing off on the job; the captains were restless; an outsider had challenged Finn two years before and had been beaten, but someone else was sure to try again and succeed. If anyone was going to take over, De Sapio felt, that right was his.

He moved characteristically slowly and carefully. First he sounded out the captains who might join him either out of disaffection for Finn or because they had become closer to De Sapio in his role as the Finn lieutenant who handled the "contracts" when Finn was absent. When the pledged support added up substantially, De Sapio moved himself and his supporters out of the Huron Club to form his own club, in a two-story building at 72 Seventh Avenue, in the heart of the Village. Since no Tammany club would be identifiable as such without an Indian name, he called it the Tamawa Club.

That fall—1937—he made a trial run for the leadership, just for organization and advertising purposes, and lost, as he expected he would. He also lost his job as secretary to the City Court judge, for the job was one allocated to the district rather than to an individual, and no district leader ever let a job he controlled stay in the possession of a rebel or rival.

However, De Sapio was back on the public payroll in the spring of 1938, despite Finn. State Supreme Court justice Louis A. Valente, doubling in brass that year as a delegate to the state constitutional convention, named De Sapio his convention clerk. It was again a patronage job, involving no work, and at half the salary of the City Court secretaryship, but it was worth many times more in terms of political significance. Valente was the political patriarch of that part of the Italian community that was Democratic. His political if not his judicial stature was enhanced by the fact that he was one of the few Supreme Court justices who took part in high Democratic councils despite the fact that judges were not supposed to be politically active. His appointment of De Sapio meant he regarded Carmine as a comer in the Italian community, a young man worth developing. In political parlance, De Sapio now had a "rabbi."

De Sapio renewed his fight against Finn from the Tamawa Club headquarters in 1939. He was now better known in the Irish community and also marked as the pride and joy of the Italians. He won the leadership fight. At least he and his followers thought they had won, and so did the newspapers, which identified him as the new leader.

The courts had ordered a new primary in the key 37th Election District because the paper ballots scattered and trodden on in the course of the September 19 riot were uncountable. The second time, with a judicial spotlight on the district, there was no vote stealing and the De Sapio slate came through with a clear majority. This in turn gave him a majority of the county committeemen from the whole First Assembly District West, and when the committee met it voted Carmine the leader. But it did not turn out to be that simple: Finn had friends at Tammany Hall.

The top Tammany leadership invoked a precedent. Many years

earlier a notoriously corrupt police captain, William S. Devery, had captured a Tammany district leadership in a primary fight. When he claimed his seat on the Tammany executive committee, he was turned down cold by boss Charles F. Murphy. Murphy, constantly fighting off various reform movements, did not want Devery's record hung around Tammany's neck, especially since the issue came up in a mayoralty election year. Murphy ruled that the Tammany executive committee, as a purely unofficial body not identified in the election law, was the sole judge of its own membership, and Murphy's stand was upheld by the courts when Devery sued for the post.

In 1939 the old court ruling was still the law, though it had not been invoked in the interim. Now it was, against De Sapio. Christopher D. Sullivan, leader of Tammany Hall, dictated that Finn, not De Sapio, would be recognized as leader and executive-committee member. There was nothing on the De Sapio record or in his background that raised the moral issue that had been used against Devery. The obstacle lay with Sullivan himself.

Christy Sullivan, a congressman from the lower East Side, who affected stiffly starched high collars and a derby hat, was exactly what he appeared—a relic of a political era long since past. His political thinking went back to the turn of the century when the "Sullivan Clan,"* of which he was a second-generation offshoot, had been the unquestioned bosses of the whole lower East Side, then the most heavily populated and politically conscious section of the city. The Sullivan name had been one to conjure with.

In 1939 Christy Sullivan was leader of Tammany Hall, but without strength in his own right. He was a figurehead for the Ahearn crowd†, who had succeeded the Sullivans as rulers of the East Side.

---

*The "Sullivan Clan" included Big Tim, Little Tim, and Florrie Sullivan. Little Tim, as a member of the state legislature, gave his name to the long-standing New York law barring the possession without a permit of concealable weapons.

†The Ahearn crowd, which controlled gambling and rackets on the lower East Side and had had a local monopoly on liquor protection during Prohibition, was headed by Edward J. Ahearn, a district leader who preferred to stay in the background and have someone else out in front as leader of Tammany Hall. He was the son of John F. Ahearn, who had been removed from office as borough president of Manhattan by Governor Hughes in 1907. The votes of the Ahearn crowd had also elected Sullivan's predecessor, James J. Dooling, as leader of Tammany Hall.

But Sullivan took himself seriously and bitterly resented the decline of Irish hegemony in Tammany affairs. Asked why he had declined to seat De Sapio, Sullivan gave reporters the excuse that he had no alternative but to stick with Finn because the latter, as sheriff, controlled 150 patronage jobs.

This reasoning was thin. Finn had neither the gumption nor the know-how to use control of those jobs as a threat to Sullivan's leadership. Sullivan was really just staving off the seating of another Italian on the Tammany executive committee, which for so long had been the almost exclusive turf of the Irish.

Tammany's racism was both conscious and unconscious. By design, there were no black district leaders. Harlem had not yet overflowed its dikes and spilled out south of 116th Street or north of 145th, or even west of Amsterdam Avenue. The territory inside its existing borders had been carefully divided among four assembly districts so that no one black segment could outvote the white territory to which it had been attached. There were a few Jewish district leaders, but the flair of the Irish for politics kept Irishmen as leaders in most of the predominantly Jewish sections. The Puerto Ricans had not yet arrived in numbers substantial enough to spread out of Spanish Harlem. The sole Italian district leader had been forced in at gunpoint in 1931.

The story was never printed in the newspapers at the time, or afterward, but Prohibition-bred mobsters operating under orders from Charles ("Lucky") Luciano—the first traceable Mafia chieftain —had walked into the office of City Clerk Harry Perry in the old Tweed Court House 100 feet north of City Hall. They told Perry, Christy Sullivan's half-brother, that he was to give up his downtown district leadership. The gunmen, significantly patting their holsters, said, "Lucky says you're through."

Perry quit, telling friends that the alternative was to have his people shot down in the street. He was succeeded by Albert Marinelli, in whose behalf Lucky's gunmen had carried the message. It was the first instance of an underworld sortie against Tammany, and it was for years the only one, but the incident left Sullivan with a personal reason for his distrust of Italians in politics.

In 1939 De Sapio might have taken the Sullivan edict in stride and just continued organizing and building up the Tamawa Club for another battle in the 1941 primary. But not so his followers, particularly the women. Somewhat to De Sapio's embarrassment, as he confessed later to friends, the De Sapio zealots took steps never before used in an intra-Tammany dispute, and which in fact were still rare for any reason in New York: they picketed.

For days and days a group from the Tamawa Club marched in front of Tammany Hall bearing signs asking: "Is Finn more important than the vote of the people?" Another set of De Sapio supporters paraded in front of the old Hall of Records on Chambers Street, in the heart of the City Hall political community, where Finn's office as sheriff was located. Their posters proclaimed: "Sheriff Finn, step down. You were defeated at the polls. The people don't want you."

The picketing was followed by an incident with both puzzling and amusing aspects. On January 3, 1940, De Sapio was appointed to his best sinecure yet, the post of secretary to General Sessions judge John J. Freschi, a fellow Village Italian, at $5,750 a year. The vacancy to which De Sapio was named had been created for that purpose by shifting the previous holder of the job, a veteran Tammany spear carrier, to a similar post in another court. De Sapio accepted, was sworn in, and two weeks later resigned. Judge Freschi explained the turnabout by saying he had confused De Sapio with De Salvio. Louis De Salvio, later a district leader himself, was at least eight inches shorter than De Sapio and weighed about half as much.

The probability was that the vacancy had been created by Tammany to buy De Sapio off and that he quit the job when he learned Finn was passing word around the First Assembly District West that it was he who had arranged for De Sapio to be on the payroll once more.

That kind of deal would have ruined the morale of the Tamawa Club workers and ended De Sapio's chances of winning a primary again. Instead, the fight went on. In 1941 it was even more bitter and hotly contested than in 1939, and again there was fraud by the Finn supporters, but without the prima facie evidence. A typical example was in the 32nd Election District, where there were nine more paper ballots in the box than there were signatures on the registry book, and the Finn forces carried the district by a margin of four votes. Since the Finn forces were in charge of the election machinery, it looked like an old-fashioned case of ballot-box stuffing. Again the affair wound up in the courts, but this time it dragged and a clear-cut majority for De Sapio in the district's county committee was not established. It probably would not have mattered anyhow, since Sullivan was still in command at the central Tammany headquarters.

But by 1943 all was changed. Mayor La Guardia had finally won permission from the state legislature, via a constitutional amendment, to reorganize the county offices in all the boroughs, and out the window went the elected sheriffs, county clerks, registers, and their many hundreds of payroll-patriot deputies. Also, Christy Sullivan was out as leader of Tammany Hall. The new forces in control were Italian. Finn, deprived of his city job, his patronage, and his backing from Tammany Hall, did not even contest the 1943 primary. He closed down the Huron Club and retired from politics.

De Sapio went in unchallenged as district leader and member of the Tammany executive committee. His Tamawa Club became the official organization for the Tammany machine in the district. It had taken him six years from his first break with Finn to scale this particular height.

THREE

THE JUNGLE

I n George Washington's first administration as President there came into being an organization which dubbed itself the Society of Tammany or the Columbian Order. It was set up as the poor man's answer to the patrician Society of the Cincinnati, a group of Washington's army officers who hoped for upper-crust rule of the new republic. Both organizations were supposedly national in scope, but the Cincinnati died off in short order, and the Society of Tammany flourished only in New York. By the Jacksonian era the patriotic order, as Tammany chose to regard itself, was synonymous with the Democratic Party of the city of New York.

The Society of Tammany had a permanent headquarters, a "hall," where the sachems and the wiskinkis donned their fraternal regalia every Fourth of July and, through district clubs with Indian names, operated the Democratic political machine the other 364 days of the year. To the people and press the machine became known as Tammany Hall, after the edifice it used to house both branches. In the first part of the current century the headquarters, or Wigwam, was a genteelly shabby structure on 14th Street east of Union Square, where Charles F. Murphy sat behind a desk and quietly issued the orders that made or broke politicians of the day.

In the late 1920s Tammany's wealth was such that it could afford a handsome, neo-Colonial brick building, tailored architecturally to its needs, at the southeast corner of 17th Street and Fourth Avenue, to house both the political and fraternal wings, with even an assembly hall for large meetings.

By 1943, when the thirty-five-year-old Carmine De Sapio first took his seat as a member of Tammany's ruling body, the executive committee, the organization was bankrupt of cash and its hall was gone, foreclosed and sold because there was no money to meet the mortgage payments. So for his first meeting, De Sapio went to a three-room suite in an office building at 331 Madison Avenue, at 43rd Street, which provided just enough space for a waiting room, a conference room, and a private office for the boss. The only political lore attached to the edifice was the fact that on a lower floor, a decade before, Louis McHenry Howe and James A. Farley had maintained the private headquarters of their drive to win delegates for the first nomination of Franklin D. Roosevelt for President.

There was no room in the new quarters for the Society of Tammany, with its banners, trophies, and souvenirs, so the "patriotic" branch of Tammany, shifting for itself for the first time, found rooms in the National Democratic Club, and later expired quietly, without even a public announcement of its dissolution.

The immediate reason for Tammany's bankruptcy in 1943 lay in La Guardia's long tenure in City Hall. His original election in 1933 had hurt Tammany, his reelections in 1937 and 1941 had ruined it. The continued hold of the fiery little mayor meant, for example, that by 1943 every city magistrate, whose term ran for ten years at most, owed his appointment to the mayor, not to Tammany Hall. The control of these police courts had been of tremendous value to Tammany in the past: favors could be done there, without fanfare or publicity, for both honest citizens down on their luck and for professional criminals who paid for protection.

The mayor had also sponsored the adoption of a new city charter, which curtailed the power of departments Tammany had always controlled. He was in the process of wiping out the county office sinecures, such as the sheriff's office and the 150 no-show jobs that went with it. There was no state patronage either, for a Republican governor, Tom Dewey, sat in Albany.

There was plenty of job and favor patronage being handed out of Washington by the third-term Roosevelt administration, but the bulk of it went to the Democratic organizations in Brooklyn and the

Bronx, in return for their steadfast support of Roosevelt's policies, compared with Tammany's opposition or sulky acceptance of them. The Bronx and Brooklyn, which once had followed Tammany's leadership for better or worse, now treated it as an errant teenager, not to be mentioned in public if possible.

All Tammany had left as a source of income and patronage were the judgeships of the elected courts, such as the Supreme, City, and Municipal benches, and the two elected Surrogates of New York County. From 1927 to 1943 it lived off these alone, staffing the courts with district leaders whose predecessors once had run whole city departments and selling nominations to the bench itself. The public knew little of this, but nominations to the Supreme Court sold for $100,000—in untraceable cash. (The fee was reduced to $75,000 in 1939, when for the first time the court salaries came under the federal income-tax laws.)

The author recalls chatting one day with the late Bert Stand, longtime secretary of Tammany and the man who knew where the bodies were buried. Using the judicial section of the city directory, known as the "Little Green Book," as a guide, the author picked off the names of the judges who he believed had bought their nominations, since they possessed no record of party or public service to otherwise justify their high rank. Stand nodded agreement with every name offered, and then added three others, to whom the author had been willing to give the benefit of the doubt. But the income from these judicial sales—at a reduced price for the lower courts—did not go to the Tammany organization. It went to groups within the Tammany wolf pack, in temporary alliance for the duration of the judicial sale.

What was even less generally known at the time was that Tammany's bankruptcy—of funds and leadership—had resulted in the passing of control of the ancient organization into the hands of the underworld, or at least that branch of the Mafia headed by Frank Costello. And no one foresaw that only two years ahead still another Mafioso, Thomas Luchese, would be able to use Tammany to set a protégé on a course that would end in his election as mayor of the greatest city of the Western world.

Like any other big-city machine, Democratic or Republican,

Tammany had always made money by protecting organized crime. It had always had its "arrangement" with professional gamblers. It once had protected organized vice as well, until leader Murphy cracked down on the practice. It furnished protection to racketeers in return for cash—a percentage of the take—plus strong-arm work at the polls on primary and election days. But the 1943 arrangement was brand-new, and it stemmed from roots planted during Prohibition.

The dry law, in effect from 1920 through 1933, had vastly expanded the area in which lawbreakers and politicians could team up profitably. It also multiplied the number of participants on both sides, since the demand for liquor rose sharply and there was little chance of an aroused public resenting those who made their liquor supply possible.

Men who drank before Prohibition continued to do so, and their concern was not with law violation, but with locating a reliable supply. Women who had never drunk, at least in public, started to in the semiprivacy and pseudo-glamour of the speakeasy. The younger generation toted hip flasks and flaunted them at college proms and football games. The illegal liquor business, operating with a vastly inflated price scale, produced greater revenue than the legal trade ever had. The "noble experiment"—as it had been termed by President Herbert Hoover—turned out to be the nation's gift to corruptionists.

In the beginning, competition for markets between rival gangs of rumrunners brought a spate of murders and created an atmosphere of violence. But by the late 1920s the trade had been organized on a big-business, noncompetitive basis. The gang chiefs parceled out territories for monopoly operation as though they were heads of big steel or electric-generator combines.

Repeal of the Eighteenth Amendment in December 1933 left the underworld unemployed, but not for long. It turned its organizational skills and manpower to racketeering. Its procedure was to demand "protection money" from businesses, small or large, just to be left unmolested. The corner vegetable store that did not pay had kerosene poured on its produce; the dry-cleaning shop was set afire; the movie theater was plagued by stinkbombs. The big manufacturer was struck, not by a legitimate labor union, but by a racket union set up to collect and then disappear. Later the racketeers moved in on the numbers game, originally a Harlem pastime, and turned it into the city-wide policy racket. Loan sharking followed, as did drug distribution.

In Manhattan, a prime area for any and all rackets, the underworld counted on the same protection by Tammany that it had enjoyed during Prohibition, and got it, for a time.

The key figures in furnishing the protection and running the rackets were James J. Hines and Lucky Luciano. Jimmy Hines was the most powerful district leader in Tammany. His own district was at the north end of Central Park, but he did not confine his operations there. He selected stooges to be leaders of the West Side and Broadway districts, which furnished most of the action, and took from them the lion's share of the protection money.

Hines's power was startlingly illustrated in 1933 when Tammany came to pick its candidate for district attorney. Tammany was under attack from all sides as a result of the Seabury investigations. It faced the loss of City Hall to La Guardia. Yet it was Hines, who made a business of protecting lawbreakers against the law, who picked Tammany's candidate for public prosecutor. With the assistance of Luciano's gorillas operating in the slum areas, Tammany stole enough votes on election day to elect Hines's man by the tiny margin of 11,000 votes in a three-way contest. The police looked the other way while gunmen took over ghetto polls and rang up illegal votes. The rackets became a public stench, but Hines's district attorney somehow could never gather any evidence.

Four years later, with La Guardia in control of the police and with the anti-Tammany forces united for a change, Tammany lost the district attorneyship to Dewey. Tom Dewey then was an ambitious young Republican who had already served two years as a special rackets prosecutor, a post to which he had been named by Governor Lehman. As special prosecutor and as district attorney, Dewey dug up plenty of evidence. He exposed Tammany's role as protector. He sent Hines and Luciano to jail. His work had the peripheral effect of creating a power vacuum within Tammany Hall. No strong district chief emerged as Hines's successor. It was a void that continued to exist until De Sapio consolidated his hold many years later.

However, the vacancy in the underworld leadership was filled without fanfare and with dispatch. A gambler and former bootlegger named Frank Costello emerged as Luciano's successor. Years later the Appalachia crime convention, broken up by a state-police raid, was to bring the underworld network into the public eye. And still later a Mafioso named Joe Valachi, in jail and terrified of being assassinated there by his own people, was to give the FBI the full story of the Mafia family system as he had learned it from the inside. But in 1939 and 1940 it was not clear that Costello, taking over control of the underworld from Luciano, was beneficiary of any foreordained system of succession. In that era there was no single name commonly used for the organized underworld. Those who knew of its existence at all referred to it simply as "the mob."

Dewey's district attorneyship made it impossible for Tammany to furnish protection for Costello and his crew. By 1941 the mob was restless enough to make a move to change the pattern. They abandoned the time-honored system of furnishing manpower and cash to support the non-Mafia men who were Tammany district leaders and decided to elect their own: it would be cheaper and more reliable.

In some districts they just made a show of force to get leaders to quit. In others they moved in on vacancies that had occurred naturally. At local meetings of county committeemen where new leaders were to be picked, groups of hard-looking characters appeared for the first time. Wearing the clothing and tools of their profession, they monitored the sessions to make sure that the "right man" was selected. It all took place as a series of isolated events, unconnected in the press and not comprehended at all by the great body of enrolled Democrats. But it amounted to a great breakthrough of the underworld into the business of politics.

By midwinter of 1941–42 the mob controlled six full votes of the Tammany executive committee out of the twelve then needed for a majority. And it was spurred to assert itself county-wide as the result of what it deemed "unfriendly" action taken by Christy Sullivan, who still hung on as leader of Tammany Hall.

La Guardia was running for a third term as mayor in 1941 and was still a formidable candidate. The reform trend which had first elected him, and which normally would have waned and died over the years, had been rejuvenated by the racket revelations. In midsummer Christy Sullivan decided it would help to lick La Guardia if he could remove the crime tag from Tammany's neck. One way to do that was for the organization to endorse the anti-racket drive by nominating for district attorney someone who had played an important part in it.

His first choice was Dewey himself. Sullivan sent two eminently respectable General Sessions Court judges to begin secret negotiations with Dewey, who by then was top boss of the GOP as well as DA. Sullivan's first offer was to give Dewey the Tammany nomination, leaving him unopposed for a second term as prosecutor. Dewey had other ideas, far beyond local office—a race for governor in 1942 to be followed by a presidential bid in 1944. He declined to run again for DA no matter how many parties nominated him.

Sullivan, undeterred, sent back word that he would accept any Dewey assistant whom Dewey suggested. Dewey named three, all Republicans. Sullivan sent the judges back to ask if Dewey did not have a Democrat on his staff who filled the bill, which would make it easier for Sullivan to get his "coup" past a probably reluctant Tammany executive committee. Dewey replied with the name of Frank S. Hogan, an independent Democrat, up to then his administrative assistant. Sullivan accepted Hogan. The executive committee went along, grumbling. The Republicans and the American Labor Party also endorsed Hogan. While the details remained secret, the author, reporting on Sullivan's gambit of 1941, was able to write in *The New York Times:*

"The political effect of the nomination of Mr. Hogan will be to weaken Mayor La Guardia and his associates on the city-wide ticket. In other words, Tammany is willing to take a plea of guilty in all of the political trials of the past six years if it can remove Mayor La Guardia from City Hall."

Sullivan's ploy failed. La Guardia was reelected, and the only consolation for his opponents was that his 133,000-vote margin of victory was the smallest since the turn of the century. In New York County, Tammany, having conceded the district attorneyship, could not even elect a borough president.

The underworld, watching from the sidelines, felt that Sullivan had thrown the ball game when he nominated a reform DA. This was the office they cared most about. There was anti-Sullivan pressure also from respectable Democrats who felt that Sullivan was a hopeless and hapless party liability. So out he went as Tammany leader, a lone figure who had lived too long politically.

When it came to picking Sullivan's successor, early tests of strength (secret and unreported) showed that the shadowy Costello owned the largest bloc of votes. These he eventually swung to Michael J. Kennedy, Jr., a young and personable congressman who was also the leader of a tiny West Side district, which entitled him to cast only one-third of a vote in the executive committee. But Costello's support elevated Kennedy to the post of principal contender. As Bert Stand later quipped to the author: "Kennedy went from one-third of a vote to six and one-third on one quick handshake."

The Costello power base within the committee acted as a magnet for otherwise unaffiliated Tammany district leaders. It attracted enough additional support from East Side and Harlem districts to put over Kennedy as leader and entrench Costello as the power behind the throne. The original six Costello votes grew into a working majority that over the years was able successively to elect Kennedy, Edward V. Loughlin, Frank Sampson, Hugo Rogers, and Carmine De Sapio as leaders of Tammany Hall.

And Costello, in the years preceding De Sapio's election as leader of the Hall, had no hesitation in exercising his power. In the fall of 1943, just as De Sapio was taking his seat as a district leader, the public got its first peek at the underworld iceberg and gasped at what it saw.

The underworld's control was revealed in connection with a judicial nomination—not one that was being sold for cash, but one that was being given away. District attorney Hogan had put a court-sanctioned wiretap on Costello's home telephone. The day after the September 1943 judicial nominating convention an agitated detective working for Hogan's office read to the DA the notes he had taken *that morning* of a conversation between city magistrate Thomas A. Aurelio and Frank Costello.

Aurelio, relatively unknown then, had been nominated the night before for the state Supreme Court, an always coveted post especially valuable in 1943 because the Democrats and Republicans had agreed in advance on a bipartisan division of the vacancies. Two Democrats and one Republican, whoever they turned out to be and regardless of their qualifications, were assured of election by being nominated on both tickets.

In the tapped phone call, Aurelio pledged Costello his "undying gratitude" and "loyalty" for his help in securing the nomination. Costello replied, "When I tell you something is in the bag, you can rest assured."

Aurelio had not paid Costello or anyone else a cent. Crassly, his potential value to Costello as a judge would have been greater on the Criminal Court, in which he sat as a magistrate, than on the Supreme Court, which tried only civil cases. It was an example—one of a few, it developed years later—of Costello using his power to promote a friendly though respectable fellow Italian. His role vis-à-vis Aurelio was like the "godfather" in Mario Puzo's later novel, and Costello enjoyed playing it.

The public did not feel that way about it. When Hogan released he transcript of the conversation to the press, the reaction was completely condemnatory. The public had evidence for the first time that an underworld king could select members of the judiciary. The fine distinction between civil and criminal court was not even discussed.

The howl from all directions was so loud that Mike Kennedy and his Republican counterpart, Tom Curran, publicly disowned the nomination, but it was too late for the bipartisan slate to be legally withdrawn or amended. The Bar Association hastily fielded an independent opponent, but Aurelio remained the official candidate of both major parties, and won easily in November. In fairness it should be said that he served his full fourteen-year term on the Supreme

Court with credit and was reelected unopposed on the basis of an unchallengeable record of probity.

But it did add up to woe for Mike Kennedy. Costello waited impatiently until right after the election, and then lowered the boom. His Tammany executive committee majority ousted Kennedy as leader to remind everybody that nobody ran out on Costello.

The nominal new leader was Edward V. Loughlin, a young lawyer from the Yorkville section of Manhattan. But the real job of running the executive committee in tandem with Costello for the next three years was in the hands of Bert Stand and Clarence Neal. Stand was a lower East Side Jew, Neal a Harlem Irishman, and both originally were members of the old Ahearn crowd. Neither was a member of "the mob," but as political pragmatists they accepted the mob's power as a fact of life.

This was the political world into which Carmine De Sapio came in 1943 as a fledgling district leader and in which he was to live for a whole decade. And he did not fight it. He voted for Loughlin, Sampson, and Rogers, supporting all of Costello's decisions until he himself became leader of Tammany Hall. His own rise could not have happened without Costello's blessing.

Many of the reservations about De Sapio's later reform tendencies were based on his record in the pre-leadership stage. For most of that period he remained a minor figure. Two far better known political animals shared with Costello the kingship of the jungle. One was Vito Marcantonio, who first dominated Spanish Harlem and then all of Harlem. The second was William O'Dwyer, first as mayor-to-be and then as mayor. Both played ball with the underworld.

Marcantonio was the New York equivalent of the old Southern Populist, a man of the people, a fighter against the "interests," a hardworking and tireless champion of the social underdog; he was also the hard-bitten dispenser of political protection to the worst elements in the community, regardless of party. He lived simply and took no money from anyone except his $10,000 a year from Congress as a member of the House. He had virtually no government allowance for staff, but managed to maintain the biggest in New York to service his all-ghetto constituency. He traded favors with the mob, not for money for himself, but for the political support that would keep him in office as the leading representative of the oppressed. He took Tammany, Republican, and Communist assistance in the same spirit.

Vito Marcantonio had entered politics as the protégé of La Guardia, who had handpicked him to be his successor in Congress when he himself became mayor. La Guardia treated him as a son, promoting his career with affection, tolerance, and even more, the practical wherewithal to support a political organization. The last consisted of instruction to the police brass that in Harlem whatever Marc said was law.

In other parts of the city the police, under La Guardia's direction, played no favorites in striking at vice and crime. In Harlem the police protected or wiped them out as Marc saw fit. There are two possible explanations for La Guardia's Harlem policy. The first is that the existence of the underworld did not shock him. He had grown up with it on the streets of the lower East Side and then in Harlem. He had used the underworld when he needed it and denounced and warred on it when he did not. He expected Marc to do the same. The second is that by the time Marc's operation was in high gear, the winning of World War II was La Guardia's principal interest in life and he paid little attention to local problems.

In following in La Guardia's footsteps, Marcantonio had first won election to Congress in the early 1930s as a Republican, from La Guardia's own Harlem district. Then he followed his mentor into the American Labor Party when it was created by the garment-trades unions in 1936. Communist infiltration into the ALP followed rapidly, and when the party-line followers gained control of the New York County branch in 1938 Marc joined forces with the Reds and became their hero and pet.

By 1942 Marc's ability to furnish protection against police interference with Harlem gamblers and loan sharks intrigued the Harlem Tammany leaders. They gave him the Democratic nomination for Congress on top of the GOP and ALP endorsements which were regularly his. The system was in full effect. He paid off the Democratic and Republican leaders alike by assuring protection for whatever rackets their "friends" wanted to run. The ALP settled for Marc's full support of the Communist party line, in or out of Congress.

Marc's alliances made his control of Harlem absolute. One Tammany district leader was once brash enough to threaten to split with him and go his own way. Marc put him in his place. "I'll run my janitor against you and beat you right in your own Democratic primary," he boasted. And he kept his word. He selected the custodian of his own clubhouse, a black man named Jim Pemberton, and elected him the Tammany district leader. No other Democrat challenged Marc for a long time.

In 1944 there was friction on the Republican side of Marc's political fence. Tom Curran appealed to his district leaders to deny Marc the Republican endorsement for Congress. He did so at the behest of the Republican high command in the state and nation, to whom Marc's Republican label and Communist party line were an embarrassing mixture. The local leaders who operated the primary-election machinery just laughed at Curran. Marc could give them more in the way of practical political rewards than the county, state, and national committees combined.

Now for the second force, William O'Dwyer. O'Dwyer was a political charmer. He had come to this country as a youth, without money, but loaded with ability and blarney. As soon as he was old enough he joined the police force and went to law school in his off hours. He practiced law in Brooklyn with little financial success, but attracted the attention of Mrs. William Randolph Hearst with work he did for her pet charity, the Milk Fund. Her influence as the wife of the important newspaper publisher got him an appointment as a city magistrate in 1932. Thereafter he went up the ladder on his own, first to Kings County judge and then to district attorney.

For a time O'Dwyer rivaled Dewey for space in the newspapers as a racket-busting DA. His most-publicized success was in convicting "Murder, Inc.," the newspaper name for a group of killers for hire. In 1941 he was the unanimous choice of the five Democratic county leaders to run for mayor against La Guardia. He lost, but his race was creditable enough for them to keep him in mind for a second try in 1945.

With that in mind, O'Dwyer took leave from his DA duties and spent World War II as a brigadier general, with duties in the field of procurement for the Army. One of those duties supplied the excuse he used when he was questioned about his first meeting with Frank Costello, in Costello's Manhattan penthouse apartment in 1942. O'Dwyer's story to investigators years later was that he had conferred with Costello to obtain his help in straightening out some Army Air Force labor problems at Wright Field, Ohio.

The political grapevine carried the story at the time it occurred, though the newspapers did not. Many of the politicians who heard it held to the belief that the meeting had not involved a conference about Wright Field or any other field. To them it was a cocktail party, and they named other underworld characters they said were present. It was their theory that O'Dwyer, who knew his Brooklyn underworld, was at least curious about the gunmen who had taken over Tammany Hall and had accepted someone's casual invitation to "come up and have a drink with Frank." The cocktail-party version was supported years later by testimony that among those present— not in any way connected with Wright Field or the Army Air Force— had been Mike Kennedy, leader of Tammany Hall; Bert Stand, its secretary, and Irving Sherman. O'Dwyer described Sherman as a close friend. J. Edgar Hoover called him "one of the most prominent criminals in the country."

O'Dwyer's record as a prosecutor of the underworld was spotty. On the plus side was his early and spectacular breaking up of the organized murder ring. On the minus side was his handling of Abe Reles. Reles was a key witness in a case involving the killing of a gangland boss, Albert Anastasia. O'Dwyer had Reles in protective custody, under twenty-four-hour guard in a fourteenth-story suite of a Coney Island hotel. Reles was found dead on the ground, killed by a fall from an open window. It was never settled whether he jumped, fell accidentally, or was pushed, but many argued that he was not the suicidal type.

Another minus involved the records of a racket-dominated Brooklyn waterfront union. John Harlan Amen, a special prosecutor of waterfront rackets, won a lengthy court battle to obtain the documents. Before he had a chance to inspect them, O'Dwyer used his superior position as the regular DA to subpoena them for himself. He admitted years later that once he had them he just sat on them, in effect suppressing the evidence. However, that exposé came years after he was out of public office, and it never handicapped him as a candidate.

O'Dwyer was remarkably astute politically. He was also well informed on city affairs and knew the problems of each of the boroughs and the neighborhoods which constituted them. His renomination in 1945 by the Democrats, plus his endorsement by Marcantonio's ALP, assured his election as mayor. Frank V. Kelly, the leader of Brooklyn, O'Dwyer's home borough, was dubious by then of O'Dwyer's reliability or stability, and his thinking influenced Ed Flynn of the Bronx, but both finally went along with O'Dwyer's supporters, James A. Roe of Queens, Loughlin of Tammany, and Jeremiah Sullivan of Richmond.

La Guardia meanwhile was furious at the Republicans and the labor leaders who had just formed the Liberal Party out of what had been the right wing of the ALP, because they made it clear that they would not support him for a fourth term. The Republicans resented La Guardia's 100 percent support of the Roosevelt New Deal, the Liberals his refusal to repudiate Marcantonio and the Communist-dominated ALP.

The Republicans and Liberals coalesced for mayor on Jonah J. Goldstein, a Tammany judge with a personal following. To make sure that they could not win with Goldstein, La Guardia deliberately divided the anti-Tammany forces by putting Newbold Morris into the race as an independent.

O'Dwyer's own, winning ticket required more explanation than was available at the time. But even then he gave a sign of the volatility of his politics that was to mark the whole five years he was in City Hall. First, he sat down with the five Democratic county leaders and came up with a city-wide ticket that was perfect as far as geographic and ethnic balance were concerned. To match O'Dwyer, the Brooklyn Irishman, the ticket included Lawrence Gerosa, a Bronx Italian, for controller and Irwin Davidson, a Manhattan Jew, for president of the City Council. All was arranged, then suddenly all was confusion.

O'Dwyer announced that the ticket he had assembled was not satisfactory, and that he would not run on it. Marcantonio backed him up, saying that the ALP would refuse to endorse it. O'Dwyer then produced, and the county leaders accepted, a substitute slate. This time the Jew on the ticket, Lazarus Joseph, came from the Bronx and was the candidate for controller, and the nominee for the City Council presidency was an Italian, Vincent Impellitteri, from Manhattan. Impellitteri's nomination staggered even the most imaginative among political reporters. A complete unknown, whose highest job had been secretary to a Supreme Court judge, was being promoted to the position of succession to the mayoralty.

Bert Stand was asked how the organization had dug him up. The Tammany secretary responded with his usual wit, but less than his usual frankness. He said that they had needed a Manhattan Italian to balance the ticket and had hunted through the city directory, the "Little Green Book," until they found one. Stand knew better then, and others did later.

The switch to a Manhattan Italian for Council president—which required a change in the controllership nominee as well, to preserve both geographic and ethnic balance—had been engineered by O'Dwyer as a favor to Marcantonio. Marc, for his part, had used his influence as a favor to another friend, Luchese. To the public Luchese was still a respectable businessman. Privately he was known to the underworld as Three Finger Brown. Under both names, he acted as though Impellitteri was his protégé.

Years later Charles Buckley, the Bronx boss, told the author exactly what had happened. At the time, Buckley was a congressman and deputy leader of the Bronx, under Flynn. Marcantonio, a fellow congressman, picked up the telephone in Buckley's congressional office in Washington, and in Buckley's presence called O'Dwyer in New York. Using the name by which O'Dwyer was familiarly known, Marcantonio said, "Bill-o, you've got to rearrange the ticket. I've got my own ginzo [vernacular for Italian] from Manhattan, Vince Impellitteri."

If Buckley knew the call had been made by Marcantonio at the request of Luchese, he did not say so. But at the time he told the author the story, in 1953, it was already a matter of record, in testimony before the State Crime Commission, that Marcantonio and Luchese were warm friends and had been so since childhood.

The fact that the outsider Luchese had the leverage to swing the deal that put Impellitteri on the city-wide ticket presaged a later fight with Costello for the overlordship of Tammany. It was also to cost the Democratic Party its whole state ticket in 1950 and to plague De Sapio in his early years as leader of Tammany Hall. But that is part of a later story.

The important thing to the Democratic leaders was to elect O'Dwyer and get the patronage they had been deprived of in the twelve long years of La Guardia. They elected O'Dwyer and his revamped ticket, and from the patronage point of view of the leaders, O'Dwyer started out 100 percent correct. On the afternoon of New Year's Eve, 1945, the five county leaders met with him in a private session at the Metropolitan Club, and brought their selections for the top city jobs along with them. The posts had previously been allocated by counties, and O'Dwyer was meeting for the first time the men he had already committed himself to appoint and would swear in to office the following day.

In the gay Metropolitan Club crowd was thirty-six-year-old Robert F. Wagner, Jr., about to leave the state assembly to accept membership on the city Tax Commission. O'Dwyer had volunteered the appointment as a gesture of goodwill to Wagner's father, the distinguished and powerful United States senator. It struck young Wagner wrong that O'Dwyer was entrusting the administration of the city's business—and his own future record—to men he did not even know. Wagner made a mental resolve that if he should ever be mayor he would make sure he knew whom he was appointing before he swore them in.

Neither Wagner nor anybody else realized he was seeing O'Dwyer at his craftiest. He was giving the patronage-starved county leaders everything they wanted, for the moment. Later, if it became necessary to threaten them to gain a point of his own, they would be more vulnerable than if they had never had the jobs in the first place. It was the beginning of a game of political cat and mouse that O'Dwyer was to play for the next five years.

FOUR

THE RISE TO THE TOP

The six years Carmine De Sapio served as a district leader of Tammany Hall before becoming the boss coincided with the era of the dirtiest politics of Tammany's long, sullied history.

In those years the underworld domination of the Democratic Party of New York County was so complete that when Mayor O'Dwyer thought the situation called for at least the appearance of reform he secretly sent the word to Costello by underworld messengers of his own. The era even witnessed the city's only election-day political murder of the twentieth century.

As De Sapio grew in experience and stature within Tammany Hall, he participated more and more in the political maneuverings either dictated by Costello or ideated by Costello's deputies on the Tammany executive committee, most of whom had identifiable underworld interests or connections. For De Sapio to have worked his way so close to the top, he had to have enjoyed Costello's favor.

Yet there was not then, or later, any appearance of a personal connection between De Sapio and the underworld rackets. Nor does the author believe any existed. To the outsider, this may appear naive. It isn't. There are ample precedents for a political boss totally immersed in corruption to keep some of his lieutenants or protégés uninvolved. The best-known instance involves Kansas City boss Tom Pendergast and the young Harry S. Truman. During the 1920s and early 1930s, Pendergast ran the most corrupt machine in America. Yet when Truman, as a Pendergast machine nominee, took over the job of county judge of Jackson County, an administrative post involving the building of roads and public buildings, Pendergast gave

Truman a completely free hand and Truman eliminated the graft which previously had been the rule for public works.

In New York there was the example of Jimmy Hines, who was the czar of the bootlegging, gambling, and racketeering protected by Tammany. Yet to represent his home district, Hines consistently sent to Congress, the state legislature, and even the Board of Aldermen, men who were completely honest, uninvolved in his protection rackets, and probably largely unaware of their extent. Hines's best-known protégé was Samuel I. Rosenman, who went on to be adviser to governors and presidents and head of the Bar Association. Rosenman started his political career as Hines's assemblyman.

In De Sapio's case, his rise within the Tammany executive committee with Costello's support was as believable as the success stories involving Truman and Rosenman, Pendergast and Hines.

In intelligence and breadth of vision, De Sapio towered above the other members of the Tammany executive committee. He had a quick wit and an easy, relaxed approach that made him popular with his peers, rather than resented as an outsider or an upstart. He voiced his opinions quietly and deferentially. He was there to lend a hand or take on a job alone if there was an organization chore to be performed. He was the senior member and unquestioned spokesman of the growing Italian bloc within the Hall. In almost every way his success within the executive committee repeated the story of his rise in the First Assembly District West. It was just the backdrop that was broader.

In 1946 he went back on the public payroll as secretary to Judge Valente, but this was just a warm-up for bigger things. Before the end of the year the executive committee picked him to be the Tammany member of the city-wide Board of Elections. The law which set up the board required that its membership consist of one Democrat and one Republican from Manhattan and one Democrat and one Republican from Brooklyn. The actual election of members was by the City Council, but it was restricted to the nominations made to it by the county committees, and in Tammany's case the county committee invariably recommended what the executive committee had decided. So basically membership on the Board of Elections was a party post, paid for out of public funds, to the tune of $10,000 a year in 1946.

Regardless of the salary, it was the most important and prestigious reward the executive committee had at its disposal, apart from the leadership of Tammany Hall itself.

De Sapio was the first district leader to represent Tammany on the Board of Elections, though the practice was common among the Brooklyn Democrats and among the Republicans from both boroughs. The nomination, ratified without dissent by the county committee and the City Council, placed De Sapio above the common herd. It made him the man to whom all other leaders had to turn for help with their problems in the primaries and general elections. He was the clearing-house through which all election-machinery patronage had to pass.

He came into this power the hard way, the indirect beneficiary of the election-day murder scandal that shook the city-wide political structure. At the center of the upheaval was Marcantonio, still the power in Harlem through his Democratic alliances even though his original patron, La Guardia, was out of politics and dying. Marc's troubles began with events over which he had no control, such as the cold war with Russia and the shooting down of American planes over Yugoslavia by the forces of Marshal Tito, then a staunch Stalin ally. Marc stuck to, or was stuck with, his Communist party line, defending the Red position and making America out the aggressor. For the first time Marc's popularity in his own congressional district declined.

Marc had real opposition for the first time in the Democratic primary, though he had full Tammany organization support. The author recalls checking by telephone with private sources at Tammany Hall on the night of the primary, to inquire about results in other areas. He found that Tammany headquarters was so busy trying to save Marcantonio's place—by juggling the paper ballots—that it had not had time to keep track of other contests.

Marcantonio lost the Republican nomination in the same primary because Dewey, entrenched as governor, had finally cracked the whip over the local Republicans, privately threatening them with investigation and exposure, and the Republican Party for the first time denied Marc its endorsement.

The election itself shaped up as a squeaker, unless something was done about it. Marc's underworld friends rallied to help him the one way they still could—organizing to steal votes on election day. In one election district they ran into an obstacle. A Republican district captain and poll watcher named Joseph Scottoriggio spurned an election-eve proposition from the mob that he take cash in return for permitting fraudulent votes to be cast the next day in his polling place. The underworld decided that if Scottoriggio would not play ball, he would not be at the polls to gum up the works, either. As he walked through the streets of Harlem early in the morning on the way to the polls, he was set upon by two thugs. Instead of just disabling him, as they probably intended, they beat him so brutally that he died. The murderers were identified by the underworld grapevine and picked up by Hogan's office on the word of stoolpigeons, but evidence that would stand up in court was never obtainable.

It was New York's first election killing in almost half a century, and in the interim the people had grown to expect law and order at the polls. The press and the public were vociferous in demanding that something be done. Marc's emergence as the election winner by the relatively narrow margin of 7,000 votes—many of them stolen—was a continuing aggravation.

The call for action against the Harlem political ring continued through the winter. In its spring session the state legislature paved the way for Marc's eventual retirement by passing the Wilson-Pakula law. Aimed directly at Marc's multipartisan political empire, the law prohibited anyone not enrolled in a particular party from entering its primary without the formal consent of the party's governing committee for the area. Thereafter Marc, an enrolled member of the ALP, could enter neither the Democratic nor Republican lists without the party's permission—which it was no longer expedient for the leadership of either major party to grant. The law was still on the books in 1970 and continued to affect major-minor party alliances.

Tammany itself had moved earlier, though less emphatically. It decided to remove the bumbling layman who represented it on the Board of Elections and who also served as the board's chairman, and replace him with a smart, sophisticated activist who was one of its own. De Sapio filled the bill completely.

Then Mayor O'Dwyer got into the act. He was subject to the pressures any mayor could expect under the circumstances. In addition, Francis Cardinal Spellman, the conservative New York head of the vehemently anti-Communist Roman Catholic Church, was indicating his disapproval via traditional church-political channels. O'Dwyer decided that the situation called for a purge that would rid Tammany of those most closely identified with Marcantonio. In practice this meant the ouster of Stand and Neal as powers behind the Tammany throne and the picking of a new leader—if only titular—to replace Loughlin.

O'Dwyer called publicly for reform. However, his behind-the-scenes emissaries sent to bring it about smelled other than of roses. He dispatched a pair of couriers to Costello, whose votes within Tammany would be needed to effect any change. One was Jim Moran, O'Dwyer's confidential agent in every office O'Dwyer ever held, but regarded by others as a collector of graft. Moran was later convicted of just that and spent seven years in Sing Sing. His companion bearer of reform tidings was Joe Adonis (Joseph Doto), owner of a café in Brooklyn frequented by the Who's Who of Brooklyn politics, and also a leading member of the Mafia. None of this—except O'Dwyer's public calls for reform—was known at the time, and much is printed here for the first time.

In the spring of 1947, while the legislature was weighing the Wilson-Pakula bill, O'Dwyer and Costello came to terms on the ousting of Loughlin and the downgrading of Stand and Neal. There was a so-called Irish bloc in the Tammany executive committee which had never joined with the Costello men. It took O'Dwyer's natural influence over this group and the votes of the hard-core Costello followers to put together a majority, since Stand and Neal had their own allies on the fringes of the Costello bloc. The news of the alliance and the

decision to carry out a change was relayed to the executive committee, waiting word at its rented headquarters, by De Sapio and Harry
Brickman, a lower East Side leader.

Brickman and De Sapio entered the meeting arm in arm and
spelled out their message of doom for the existing leadership. It mattered little to Loughlin, who took his title casually. But it was a bitter
pill for Stand and Neal. They had been thinking of De Sapio as the
potential new leader, but as their own ally, in the event they had to
toss Loughlin to the wolves. Instead, the temporary alliance of Costello and the Irish bloc elected O'Dwyer's choice, Frank J. Sampson.

The shift of the titular leadership from Loughlin to Sampson
eliminated Stand and Neal as the chief Tammany manipulators, just
as O'Dwyer had planned, but it did not shake Costello's grip. The
real duties of leadership gravitated to a quartet, Francis X. Mancuso,
Sidney Moses, Brickman, and De Sapio. They acted as a directorate
similar to the famed Albany regency which had run Democratic politics in the state in the days of Martin Van Buren.

Of De Sapio's fellow directors, the senior member and informal
chairman was Mancuso, known as "the Indian" because of his ruddy
complexion and beaklike nose. He had been a judge of the Court of
General Sessions, a high criminal court, until he resigned under an
indictment that stemmed from his connection with a bank that failed
in 1929. In the years that followed he was widely recognized as a link
between Tammany and the underworld. Sidney Moses had been accused by primary-election opponents of having connections with loan
sharking, strictly a mob operation. Brickman, shifty-eyed and the
constant wearer of a look of apprehension, had become an East Side
leader only after the mob had assumed control of that area's politics.

Individually or together, they were sleazy company for De Sapio.
But if he thought so, he never said it or showed it. He played the
game, the only one in town.

The transfer of power had no effect at all on Tammany's alliance
with Marc. In 1948, when it perforce had to name a candidate of its
own to oppose him in the general election, its heart was not in winning and the directorate scanned the list of potential nominees, looking for the surest loser. At a Tammany luncheon gathering Mancuso,

Moses, Brickman, and De Sapio collectively challenged the author, then a political reporter, to "guess who we've stuck with running against Marc." They laughed as they named the man, a less than bright member of their own executive committee.

As for O'Dwyer, he blew alternately hot and cold on Tammany, accepting the directorate's recommendations one month, denouncing them the next. Sampson was a sideline figure in the game, but De Sapio was in the middle of the action.

Sampson's lack of real power showed up toward the end of his first year in the job. In the spring of 1948 he expressed reservations about the candidate picked to oppose Marcantonio, but was overruled. Later, when Harry S. Truman looked like a sure loser for the presidency in the fall, individual Tammany district leaders pressed for the right to accept ALP endorsements, where obtainable, for their local candidates, to avoid their being dragged down in an anti-Truman landslide. With such dual endorsement they would benefit from the votes cast for Truman and also from those for Henry A. Wallace, whose Progressive Party was represented in New York by the ALP. Sampson balked at accepting the ALP again as a public ally, and again he was overruled. There were many other unpublicized differences between the titular leader and the majority bloc.

The political dirt began to fly publicly when a division occurred over the nomination to the Surrogate Court of New York County, an office dear to Tammany's heart because of the patronage for lawyers that the Surrogate controlled. De Sapio was right in the middle of this one.

The directorate toyed with the idea of nominating Supreme Court justice Louis A. Valente, De Sapio's original political angel, for Surrogate. But he was too old, too close to mandatory retirement. So they settled for his nephew, General Sessions judge Francis A. Valente, younger and much less identified as a political judge. De Sapio presided over a rare luncheon caucus of the majority, personally picked up the tab, and then shepherded the votes to the Tammany headquarters to make the result official, over the hot protests of the Irish bloc.

There was an immediate reaction from O'Dwyer, possibly because the mechanics of the selection so publicly downgraded Sampson, the titular leader. More likely, it was because the selection of a Valente would take the cherished guardianship of infants and estates out of Irish-Catholic hands, in which it had always rested, and turn it over to the less church-conscious Italians.

O'Dwyer's first step was to have his adroit press secretary leak to a gullible reporter a story that there was proof that three Harlem district leaders had been paid $1,000 each to cast their votes for the younger Valente. The story, printed under big headlines, was picked up by most of the other papers, but it was a complete hoax. The three leaders named all belonged to the ruling majority and did not have to be bought. And if money had to be used, $1,000 was a pittance, nothing like what deadlock-breaking votes for that particular office would have been worth. Furthermore, no proof existed. But the yarn served its purpose. Every member of the executive committee was subpoenaed to Hogan's office, with much publicity, and the mantle of corruption was once more draped around Tammany's neck.

O'Dwyer followed this sneak punch with a full-scale, open denunciation, calling Tammany "a cesspool of corruption." He said he would put up his own candidate for Surrogate in the primary. For this, with typical craftiness, he selected another Italian, Vincent Impellitteri, president of the City Council, as a stand-in.

The Tammany directorate, on orders from Costello, retaliated by ousting Sampson from his titular leadership and replacing him with Hugo B. Rogers, borough president of Manhattan. The author received a telephone call from a Tammany district leader several days in advance, tipping him off to the impending change. The story was printed and turned out to be correct. This was not strange, since the district leader in question, though of no apparent stature in the Hall, had always been accurate in tips he saw fit to pass along. What was puzzling was how he knew so much, so often. The mystery was cleared up several years later when testimony before the Kefauver Committee identified him as the man who carried the messages from Costello to Tammany Hall.

Mayor O'Dwyer, in retaliation for the dumping of Sampson,

fired two Tammany district leaders who had city jobs and continued to make additional anti-Tammany noises. But it was camouflage. The arrangements for peaceful settlement had already been made.

The mayor accepted the selection of Borough President Rogers as Tammany leader with the warmth he would have shown to any other of his colleagues on the Board of Estimate, then the city's real governing body. O'Dwyer also withdrew Impellitteri as his candidate for Surrogate. Tammany in turn withdrew Valente and as a face-saving device accepted from O'Dwyer a panel of three Irish judges from among whom Tammany could pick the compromise nominee. Both Valente and the compromise choice, John A. Mullen, had eminently respectable judicial records, but the stench raised by the split and by the charges and countercharges lingered so long that Mullen lost in the November election to a Republican-Liberal coalition candidate.

The result of all the shooting was that Tammany lost the valuable Surrogate Court patronage, O'Dwyer no longer had the foothold within Tammany that the Sampson leadership had represented, and Costello's grip, exercised through Rogers, grew tighter than ever.

During the Rogers regime, which covered the period from July 1948 to May 1949, Mancuso, as senior member of the directorate and spokesman for Costello, could be seen daily at the Tammany headquarters, giving Rogers orders or exercising the power directly if Rogers was busy downtown in his borough president's office. When Rogers himself went out as leader, and lost the borough presidency to boot, he told the press: "I have been a sacrificial lamb in a game of political chess." Mixed metaphor or no, seldom has a politician spoken truer words.

Rogers' ouster, which was followed by the election of De Sapio, came in the summer of 1949. With a mayoralty election scheduled for the fall, O'Dwyer found it good tactics to present himself again as an anti-Tammany mayor. He started out by playing footsie publicly with the Fair Deal Democrats, a fledgling reform group which was an offshoot of the New York Young Democratic Club. Although its ranks were filled with eager young Democrats, it did not shape up as a real rival for Tammany. On the evening that Tammany held its annual fund-raising dinner, the mayor, who had been invited to attend, chose to spend the time seven blocks south in another hotel, lecturing the Fair Deal Democrats on the virtues and necessity of political reform. He held off his heavy anti-Tammany artillery until late May, following the city's most spectacular election for Congress, in which Tammany suffered a body blow.

A congressional seat on Manhattan's West Side, in a district stretching from Chelsea to Washington Heights, had come up for grabs as a result of the death of Sol Bloom, a millionaire sheet-music and theatrical entrepreneur who had turned the district Democratic and had become its U.S. representative in seeming perpetuity. Franklin D. Roosevelt, Jr., the son of the late President, decided to go after the congressional seat to launch his own political career. He was a natural for the spot, and it for him, even though he lived in DutchessCounty, the Roosevelt family's ancestral bailiwick. The law permitted Roosevelt to run so long as he moved into the area before election day.

The West Side Irish leaders could have courted young Roosevelt and made him their debtor. Instead, they pigheadedly turned him down cold as an outsider. Bert Stand, sitting on the periphery of the meeting, as did the other members of the executive committee, contributed the classic mot: "Look fellows, it is none of my business, outside my district. But why don't you take Roosevelt? You might need a character witness some day."

Roosevelt's candidacy was immediately adopted by the astute Alex Rose of the Liberal Party, and Roosevelt ran as well on an independent line labeled the Fair Deal Party. The opposition consisted of separate tickets fielded by Tammany Hall, the Republicans, and the ALP. Roosevelt was theoretically the underdog, but the handsome bearer of what was then still the greatest name in American politics drew big crowds at every street-corner rally. Every hour of every day for more than three weeks loudspeakers blasted forth on the issues, as seen by all four nominees.

When the shouting was over, nearly 60 percent of the voters— an unprecedented percentage for a special election—had gone to the polls, and more than half voted for young Roosevelt. His clear majority over the combined vote of his rivals clearly indicated how low was the estate of the political machine. The result was another black eye for Tammany, even though the decision to turn down Roosevelt had been the local leadership's, rather than that of the ruling clique. Again, it was time for demands for a change. And again, O'Dwyer took the lead.

In late July, as the Democratic organizations all over the city were in the throes of nominating their borough tickets as well as renaming O'Dwyer, Joseph, and Impellitteri for the city-wide slate, O'Dwyer publicly demanded the resignation of Rogers as leader of Tammany Hall and the naming of someone other than Rogers as the candidate for Manhattan borough president. The organizations had no course other than to submit. They could not fight O'Dwyer for renomination for mayor and hope to win. Neither could they support him for mayor and defy him on the leadership and borough presidency.

The directorate—Mancuso, Moses, Brickman, and De Sapio—met before the executive committee convened at Tammany Hall on the afternoon of July 20, 1949, and came out of their huddle with the recommendation of De Sapio for leader of Tammany Hall. At the same time they put up a dummy candidate for borough president, who would be withdrawn when a final selection could be made under the new leader. They also endorsed the city-wide O'Dwyer slate for reelection.

The resolution which recognized De Sapio as leader of Tammany Hall drew no negative votes in the executive committee meeting that followed immediately, but the eight-member bloc of West Side Irish, entitled to cast three full votes on the executive committee, abstained. So De Sapio was leader, elected by the votes of those whose basic allegiance was to Frank Costello of the Mafia. In this De Sapio was no different from Kennedy, Loughlin, Sampson, or Rogers, as far as external indications were concerned. Beneath the surface there was a vast difference: Costello had decided to turn reformer. If the story had been printed at the time, no one would have believed it. But it is true, and is worth telling now.

The one-time bootlegger and gambling czar was rich. He had

his penthouse apartment in Manhattan, his estate at Sands Point on Long Island. His money continued to roll in from gambling enterprises in Louisiana and Nevada, and he needed none from New York. He had been privately seeing a leading psychoanalyst, something the author discovered via a friend who visited the same doctor, and was seeking to attain a quiet life and the respectability of a member of the establishment. But his efforts had been, thus far, to no avail.

For example, there was his attempt to raise funds for charity. Costello had given the Salvation Army a large cash gift in 1948, and when the 1949 fund drive started he was one of two hundred previous big donors who were honored with the title "vice-chairman" of the campaign. Whoever filled out the parchment certificate at the Salvation Army or at its fund-raising agency did not know one Frank Costello from another. Costello, however, took his title seriously, the first he had ever got from the upper world. He paid for engraved invitations which read:

Dinner and Entertainment
Sponsored by
Frank Costello
Vice-chairman of Men's Division
Salvation Army Campaign
Monday, January 24, 1949, at 6:30 p.m.
At the Copacabana
10 East 60th Street, New York
Entire Proceeds for
Salvation Army Association
$100 per person   Dress Informal

The invitations went out to all the political leaders and judges Costello knew, and nearly all of them came. Hugo Rogers, De Sapio, most of the members of the executive committee were there, as well as people like Howard Chandler Christy, the illustrator. The advance sale alone raised more than $10,000. But someone who had been invited, and was not going, tipped off the press that there was a party at the Copacabana, given by *the* Frank Costello, and it might be worth their while to check on who attended. So Costello's reward was a series of raised-eyebrow stories in the press and embarrassment for his friends over the company they kept. By the following nightfall he had resigned his fund-raising vice-chairmanship.

Then came the case of his dentist, a respectable citizen with an itch to serve in government. Costello recommended him to Tammany, and Tammany had forwarded the name, with its blessings, to the Truman administration in Washington, for appointment as head of the U.S. Government Assay Office in New York. The appointment was all set until someone discovered that the nominee had been recommended because he filled Costello's cavities. The administration ran for cover, and the nomination was withdrawn.

These two episodes convinced Costello that his influence was a liability rather than an asset; that public affairs could not give him the respectability he yearned for. And Tammany could not give him anything else that he wanted or needed.

There is no proof that Costello and De Sapio ever sat down face to face and discussed the latter's accession to the leadership of Tammany Hall. In 1951, under oath before an investigating committee which delved into the relationship between crime and politics, they admitted knowing each other and swore the relationship was casual. It had to have been more than that, in view of the closeness of the Tammany directorate—of which De Sapio was a member—and Costello in the years directly preceding De Sapio's election.

In 1949, however, the actual control Costello had within Tammany was more a matter of speculation than proven fact, as far as the public was concerned. De Sapio, from the point of view of Costello and also the general public, was respectable. And here was Costello, wanting to wash his hands of the whole Tammany mess, with a respectable young Italian-American waiting on the sidelines who had earned the right to leadership. But handing over the leadership without a guarantee of continued support would have been ridiculous.

Everything which happened then and later supports the idea that Costello said something like this to De Sapio: "You're a nice young guy with a future. I'm going to tell the boys to put you in as leader. Let the rackets take care of themselves. Keep your own nose clean. The Italians in politics have been smeared by all these investigations. You can restore the Italian name in politics by running a good clean show. You'll get no interference from me, and if you need any help in keeping the boys in line, let me know."

If Costello did not say that face to face with De Sapio, he acted thereafter as though he had. And so did De Sapio. From his first week as leader, he was off and running to create that new image that Tammany needed so badly.

FIVE

THE TASTE OF POWER

There are no indications that Costello ever interfered with De Sapio's leadership, but there are several which hint that he actively supported De Sapio's new crusade for political reform and for a new political image that reform might bring.

De Sapio's first exercise of his grant of power was to abolish the directorate of which he had been a member, an act for which he needed Costello's approval. He chopped off the authority of the other three and made it clear, to them and to the public, that he alone was leader of Tammany Hall. On his second day at the desk reserved for the boss in Tammany headquarters, he issued a formal statement that his own election proved that he had not been the choice of any clique or faction, since no votes had been cast in the negative. He tossed in without documentation the assertion that he had been, however, actively opposed by "Mancuso, Clarence Neal and Company."

"Upon my election my first act was to demand the resignation of Francis X. Mancuso as chairman of the elections committee," read the De Sapio communiqué. "I have received it. I am sincerely convinced that my election will destroy the last vestiges of the influence of this group in the Democratic Party in New York County."

Mancuso, his Indian beak definitely out of joint, grumbled to the press that he had written his letter of resignation before De Sapio had asked for it; that he had no connection with Neal; and that he did not know "what Mr. De Sapio means by 'and Company.' " Neal, who had been Stand's partner earlier, by this time was already on the sidelines.

Brickman, whose previous prominence carried with it no official title, was just ignored, which had the same effect as firing him. He and Mancuso were later to bob up again, as avowed enemies of De Sapio. Sidney Moses, the most personable of the trio, was allowed to resign as secretary of Tammany Hall with a graceful note saying that the leader should have the chance to pick his own principal aide. De Sapio filled the vacancy with an old friend from his Tamawa Club.

In answering questions from the press as he took over the leadership, De Sapio took the position on his relationship with Costello that he maintained ever after. It was that he knew Costello and had met him on several occasions, but that the two had never discussed politics. "Will Mr. Costello have any influence in Tammany Hall?" he was asked by a reporter who remembered the Aurelio case six years before. "Decidedly not," De Sapio replied with deliberate emphasis.

De Sapio preferred to be accepted on the basis of that portion of his prepared statement which read: "The traditions of the Democratic Party were built on the humane and liberal records of men like Governor Alfred E. Smith, President Franklin Delano Roosevelt, Governor Herbert Lehman, Senator Robert F. Wagner, and President Truman. It is to the ideals and aims of these men that the Democratic Party in this county will remain loyal."

The names were those that any Democratic leader anywhere in New York state would count off as a party platform on any necessary occasion. However, De Sapio immediately followed his words with action that linked his own leadership—and Tammany—with the political fortunes of the distinguished name-bearer most available, young Robert F. Wagner, Jr.

De Sapio was able to hook up with history as fast as he did because one of the problems lying on his desk was the selection of a new candidate for borough president of Manhattan. Hugo Rogers, when he resigned the week before as leader of Tammany, had hoped to hang on to his borough presidency. While he had been given some encouraging words on which he based his hope, no one took the idea seriously.

But Tammany needed the borough presidency. The office was a job haven for half a dozen Tammany district leaders; the borough's corps of 1,200 highway laborers, truck drivers, and sewer maintainers included many noncompetitive civil service positions, and these were filled with Tammany election-district captains.

For the election ahead, the Republicans and the Liberal Party were already united on a city-wide, anti-Tammany fusion ticket, headed by Newbold Morris, La Guardia's former protegé, for mayor. They were expected to round out their union by nominating the Republican Oren Root for Manhattan borough president. Root had achieved much prominence when he formed the independent clubs for Wendell L. Willkie in 1940, and he loomed as a formidable opponent for any routine Tammany nominee.

De Sapio announced he was not considering Rogers for reelection and turned quietly to young Wagner. He knew, on the basis of conversations with Alex Rose of the Liberal Party, that the Wagner candidacy, owing to the preeminence of the Wagner name in labor and liberal circles, would break up the coalition behind Root and create a Democratic-Liberal coalition behind Wagner.

The junior Wagner, then thirty-nine years old, had served as an assemblyman just before World War II and during the war had been an air intelligence officer in North Africa. Starting in 1946 he was pushed steadily ahead in city government by O'Dwyer. The mayor first made him a member of the Tax Commission, then commissioner of the Department of Housing and Buildings, then chairman of the City Planning Commission. In all these capacities Wagner had served without greatly distinguishing himself, or getting into trouble.

The operation that led to Wagner's endorsement as the joint nominee of the Democratic and Liberal parties in Manhattan, while they remained opponents city-wide, bore the hallmark of De Sapio's craftsmanship.

First, it was arranged that the Liberal Party would formally announce that it was prepared to back Wagner if Tammany did, but that otherwise it would nominate Root. This contrived ultimatum gave De Sapio a sound position from which to talk down possible

81

opposition within the Tammany executive committee. Second, Wagner issued a statement that he was prepared to run as the Democratic-Liberal nominee "with the understanding that when elected I shall have a free hand in organizing the office of borough president and in discharging the duties of that office."

Wagner thus said that Tammany could no longer count on staffing the office as it had in the past. At the same time De Sapio was able to give confident assurances to the Tammany executive committee that they should not be too alarmed because Wagner was, after all, an organization Democrat.

De Sapio, Wagner, and Alex Rose had worked out a deal, spelled out only among themselves, and revealed here for the first time. As a token of Liberal Party prestige, Rose was to name one man for a job in the borough president's office. Also, as a concession to the Liberal Party and the editorial writers, no Tammany district leader would be named commissioner of borough works, the top appointive job in the office. The commissioner had considerable authority and became acting borough president when the elected head was away. On the other hand, De Sapio would furnish Wagner with names of district leaders or other organization nominees as candidates for the remaining "political" jobs in the office. The nominees would be men and women who could be counted on to reflect credit on the office and the organization, and Wagner would appoint them if he agreed they filled the bill.

It is worth looking back to see how the deal worked out. For example, Rogers' borough works commissioner had been Philip Zichello, not a district leader. Zichello, in no way personally disreputable, nevertheless owed his political post to the fact that he was the brother-in-law of a mobster named Willie Moretti, later the corpse in a spectacular gangland killing. Wagner's selection, recommended by De Sapio, was Charles S. Hand, a distinguished newspaperman for decades before he went into government. Hand first had been Jimmy Walker's secretary in City Hall and then his sanitation commissioner. He had emerged clean from the Seabury investigations, and was a veteran campaign publicist who enjoyed the friendship of all who knew him, including members of the Tammany executive committee.

The assistant commissioner under Rogers had been Harry Brickman, in recognition of his service as a member of the Tammany directorate. In Brickman's place De Sapio proposed George W. Thompson, whom Wagner named. Thompson, like Brickman, was a district leader, but Thompson got there by fighting the mob, not playing ball with it. Moreover Thompson, a product of tough steamfitters-union politics, was ideal for handling the laborers and pavers, which the job involved.

All the way down the line the story was similar. One civil service engineer, who had been upgraded to chief engineer because he was a district leader, reverted to civil service rank and was replaced by an equally political civil service engineer who was not a district leader. Two other leaders, who held small jobs befitting their relatively low standing in politics, retained them. District leader Sal Titolo, a voting member of the Costello–De Sapio bloc, was replaced by Herman Weinkrantz, the Liberal Party man chosen by Rose. So when the shooting was over and the smoke had cleared, Tammany had really lost one job in the office—Titolo's—but the whole setup looked better to the public.

Wagner's two personal appointments, of Nelson Seitel as executive manager and Stanley H. Lowell as assistant to the president, were two jobs normally reserved for those having a confidential relationship with the borough president. Both were subsequently to serve Wagner long and well in the mayor's office.

De Sapio had recommended Hand for the top appointive post in the borough president's office in order to help build up Wagner as a public figure in his own right, on top of the prestige he inherited from the family name. Showing that interest in the long-range approach which was to mark his entire career as a top political leader, De Sapio wanted his first political selection as Boss to look good from the start and even better with the passage of time. His tactics, however, were low-keyed, and sometimes months went by between a De Sapio decision and the first signs of implementation.

Tammany had always combined ritual with its political decisions. A man privately selected for some high public office would be given "exposure" before his selection became public, by being placed prominently on the dais at an important dinner or being assigned the seconding speech for some other nominee many months in advance. The word thus passed through the Tammany organization.

The author got an intimate view of how De Sapio operated within this framework in the spring of 1952, when Hand died in office. The Tammany organization was in charge of the arrangements for the funeral, which was held at St. Patrick's Cathedral. The author, who intended to attend as a friend and mourner, was invited to be an honorary pallbearer. He accepted, and at the ceremony made a mental note that he was the only active newspaperman so selected, although a number of others would have qualified. It looked like a "buildup," but why?

A month later De Sapio asked the author to be Hand's successor. It became clear that De Sapio had made his selection at the time of Hand's death but held off its implementation until the period of mourning had passed. Furthermore, when he declined the honor, De Sapio doggedly refused to accept the refusal as final. He kept the place open for three additional months, before he broke down the author's reluctance to leave the newspaper business.

At no time during Wagner's first three years as borough president was the Wagner–De Sapio relationship really intimate. Yet it was typical that when a job was available—as in the case of choosing Hand's successor—De Sapio would cast about for the candidate, do the actual recruiting, and present his case to Wagner for approval. Wagner was ever cautious of his own name and reputation. De Sapio played up to this caution by presenting only names he knew Wagner would want to hear.

The abolition of the directorate and the cleaning up of the borough president's office still left Marcantonio a thorn in Tammany's side. It was removed at the first opportunity. In contrast with 1948, when De Sapio had been party to picking a Tammany candidate easy for Marc to defeat, in 1950 he set in motion forces which made Marc's downfall inevitable.

De Sapio sat down with Tom Curran, his Republican opposite number, and with Murray Baron, the titular Liberal Party head in New York County, and worked out an agreement that the three parties would gang up on Marc by naming a single candidate to oppose him. After some bickering on personalities and ideologies, they agreed on a conservative Tammany state senator, James G. Donovan. On election day 1950 the coalition behind Donovan beat Marcantonio, running this time on the ALP line alone, by 50,000 to 36,000, ending the career of a man who for so long had represented ghetto politics at both its best and worst. O'Dwyer, still mayor at the time the coalition was worked out, wired De Sapio his "heartiest congratulations."

While De Sapio had been busy during 1949 with his vacuum cleaning and window washing in Tammany, Bill-o had been equally active upsetting the political applecart in the city as a whole.

As he approached the end of his first term, O'Dwyer enjoyed the reputation of having been a good mayor. He had earned it. When he was concentrating on government problems in City Hall rather than on political gamesmanship, he worked hard and intelligently and produced results. Two dozen of the principal civic and good-government organizations in the city, ordinarily slow to praise an organization-Democrat mayor, had united in giving O'Dwyer a testimonial dinner at the end of his first two years. They had said lovely things about his administration which he could quote in a campaign and which nobody could deny.

Thus he was a natural for reelection, even though the Republican and Liberal parties were joining hands in opposition. No one took O'Dwyer seriously when he announced he would not run for a second term. He was, everyone assumed, inviting a draft, a political ploy usually arranged by the candidate himself to make it appear that the office was seeking the man.

Organized labor, to which the O'Dwyer administration had been friendly and generous, furnished the cadres for the draft movement, and the political community, thinking of no nominee but O'Dwyer, sat back and waited for him to say yes the second time he was asked. He flabbergasted everyone by again saying no. He lent authenticity to his renunciation by leaking word to District Attorney Hogan and to Francis L. Valente, whose Surrogate candidacy he had aborted the year before, that he would support them for the nomination in his stead. The pledges of support were, of course, contradictory. He could be for one or the other, but not both. But then O'Dwyer himself was a constant contradiction.

He was jealous of his good name. So jealous that he deposed John Cashmore as Kings County Democratic leader because Cashmore permitted a minor scandal in the Police Department to be developed by Brooklyn prosecutors into a widely advertised exposé of police protection of the policy racket. And so jealous that before he permitted the Brooklyn Democrats to endorse a Brooklyn Republican for a Supreme Court vacancy he made the man in question issue a public retraction of things he had said critical of O'Dwyer's record as district attorney.

Yet he kept Moran, whom numerous people warned him about, as his closest associate. He gave Moran what amounted to a license to steal, first from a Fire Department sinecure, and later rewarding him further by naming him to what was supposed to be a lifetime job on the Board of Water Supply. O'Dwyer kept the itching fingers of professional politicians out of the police rackets but allowed his own old friends in the department to do as they pleased. He would denounce Tammany and the underworld whenever it suited his purpose, but kept his own connections with them alive and current.

O'Dwyer liked the power that went with the mayoralty, yet he acted as though he feared the spotlight would search out some vulnerable point in his own past. This ambivalence about the mayoralty was not new. In 1945, when he was about to become the candidate, with election assured, he privately inquired if he could not get a State Supreme Court nomination, the only loophole for belated withdrawal from the race for someone already nominated in the primary. Even before that point had been reached, he told one county leader that he would not take the nomination on a silver platter, and told another—the same day—that if the bosses did not name him he would run in the primary anyhow.

In early summer of 1949, with O'Dwyer reiterating his decision not to seek a second term, three of the five Democratic county leaders believed him; they accepted his decision and cast about for a substitute. The three, Rogers of Tammany, Roe of Queens, and Sullivan of Richmond, voted to nominate District Attorney Hogan.

Flynn of the Bronx had other thoughts, which he kept to himself, that O'Dwyer could still be persuaded to run if he could be assured that he would not have to serve out the full four years of his second term.

And this could have advantages for the Democratic Party. For instance, if O'Dwyer ran and was reelected in 1949 but resigned in 1950 to accept appointment to some high federal post, there would have to be a mayoral election in 1950 for the balance of O'Dwyer's term. And since 1950 was also a gubernatorial election year, the holding of a mayoral election at the same time would help bring out the Democratic vote in New York City and give the Democrats a chance to recapture the governorship, held eight years by Dewey.

In the post-O'Dwyer years, many people thought that O'Dwyer had resigned during his second term because he feared scandals looming ahead. What they did not know was that his resignation had been arranged even before he ran for his second term.

While the other county leaders were still counting off a "will he, won't he run" game, Flynn arranged for O'Dwyer to meet with President Truman in the White House and for Truman to offer O'Dwyer an appointment as Ambassador to Mexico, effective in August 1950, at the end of eight months of the mayoral term. It was a tempting offer to O'Dwyer, who liked the Mexican climate and whose brother had an Arizona ranch.

It took someone of Flynn's stature to make the arrangement, for O'Dwyer had been the head man in a Ditch Truman movement among Democrats prior to the 1948 nominating convention, when Truman's chances of reelection looked slender. At the time Truman, a good hater, had used some old-fashioned Missouri mule-skinner words to describe O'Dwyer's conduct. But the urbane Flynn, confidant and intimate of the late Franklin Roosevelt, and respected by Truman for his political acumen, turned the trick. He convinced Truman that the razzle-dazzle would help the New York Democrats elect a governor and that Truman, as a good party man, should forgive O'Dwyer's disloyalty.

O'Dwyer came back from Washington with Truman's private promise of the ambassadorship, to be his at the agreed time provided he followed the Flynn script. After a midnight session with Flynn and Cashmore of Brooklyn at Gracie Mansion, O'Dwyer announced he had changed his mind and was a candidate for reelection as mayor.

With the assurance that no one other than the quartet of insiders knew that his new commitment had a time limit, O'Dwyer said with a perfectly straight face: "Only when it became apparent that Tammany Hall was conniving to gain control of the city and its resources did my course become clear and compelling. I deem it my duty in the best interests of the city to run for reelection. I specifically reject the support of the sinister elements of Tammany Hall. My appeal is to the decent citizens of every party."

O'Dwyer was doing a figure-eight on particularly thin ice, since he was on record as supporting Hogan as his political successor, and Hogan was also Tammany's selection. The mayor apologized the best he could for shunting aside Hogan by saying that Hogan had not been the unanimous choice of the county leaders—O'Dwyer's own men, however, having been the dissenters—and that no reflection on the Manhattan district attorney was intended.

Even after his reelection, and with the knowledge that he would be able to leave the mayoralty gracefully not too far in the future, O'Dwyer continued to exercise his schizophrenic approach to the job. While hospitalized with a virus attack in December 1949 he filed his retirement papers with the New York City Retirement Board, documents which constituted his resignation from the mayorality to which he had been reelected only the month before. Jim Moran on his own initiative tore down to the board's office and retrieved the supposedly irrevocable documents. He took them back to O'Dwyer's hospital bedside and burned them in the mayor's view.

It was a crass display of Moran's hold on O'Dwyer, and as such, was never admitted to have occurred. It would not even have been picked up by the acute microphones of the political grapevine had not Moran, in waving the burning sheets of paper, set fire to the window curtains, necessitating the calling of the fire department.

The whole series of incidents taught De Sapio several lessons. One was that things were not necessarily the way they seemed on a city-wide basis any more than they were on a district or county basis.

A second was that Flynn had the real power in New York Democratic politics, even though the carefree Bronx boss seldom chose to exercise it. De Sapio gravitated into the Flynn orbit, for several good reasons. A working relationship was natural enough—more natural than with any other county leader, since there were party nominations for the State Supreme Court which had to be made jointly by the Bronx and Tammany machines. In addition, De Sapio liked and admired Flynn and his political tactics which eschewed graft and pettiness and played for the long run.*

And Flynn, for his part, grew to like and admire De Sapio. He told friends that in all the years since 1924, when Boss Murphy died, De Sapio was the first Tammany leader with whom he could sit down and discuss a political problem in a friendly, rational manner. De Sapio played the role of junior partner, in keeping with his tactful approach to almost anything or anybody. Flynn, though he seldom elected to throw his weight around, was the big-time leader De Sapio intended someday to be. As a result, it was Flynn rather than De Sapio who bore the real responsibility for what turned out to be the election fiasco of 1950.

O'Dwyer and his running mates, Controller Lazarus Joseph and City Council President Vincent Impellitteri, had won the 1949 election easily over Newbold Morris, the Republican-Liberal nominee, and Marcantonio, running on the ALP ticket. Then O'Dwyer resigned on schedule in August 1950, leaving Impellitteri as acting mayor.

Flynn had meanwhile worked out with Alex Rose his plans for what would come next in the dual mayoralty-gubernatorial campaign. For mayor, the Democratic and Liberal parties would nominate State Supreme Court justice Ferdinand Pecora, a staunch New Deal Democrat who had an additional appeal to the Liberal Party leadership because he and David Dubinsky, the labor leader whose

*Flynn was unjustly smeared by the "Bronx paving-block scandal," in which he was accused of confiscating $250 worth of old paving blocks and using city labor to beautify a courtyard on his Lake Mahopac estate. The incident came to light only because Flynn, discovering from his wife's landscape architect that city property had been used in his behalf, tried to pay the city for the work. It was the only time in Flynn's career that he was accused of dishonesty.

garment union was the Liberal Party mainstay, were close friends and gin-rummy opponents.

The candidate for the U.S. Senate would be the incumbent Herbert Lehman, four-time governor and pillar of the Democratic Party, who had won the Senate seat the year before to fill a short-term vacancy. His ties with the garment trade unions were impeccable.

The Liberals would support any one of three Irish Catholics whom the Democrats picked for governor from a panel consisting of Court of Appeals judge Albert Conway of Brooklyn, Supreme Court justice Charles S. Desmond of Buffalo, and Congressman Walter A. Lynch of the Bronx. The Democratic leaders chose Conway. On paper it was a dream ticket—an Italian Protestant for mayor, the idol of the Jews for U.S. Senator, and a respectable organization Irish-Catholic Democrat for governor. But the ticket started falling apart even before it was official.

Conway, though he had got his start in Franklin Roosevelt's state administration, had been an ultraconservative judge on the Court of Appeals. The day after the political leaders announced their selection of Conway, Louis Hollander, head of the CIO Council of Greater New York, blasted Conway as a reactionary and a labor baiter. Hollander spoke for a far greater chunk of organized labor than did the Liberal Party. When he fired his salvo, the Conway candidacy sank, and the judge hastily withdrew consideration of his name by the convention.

Flynn and his associates from around the state had to pick a new candidate. They decided on Lynch, since Desmond was not well known. Flynn later told the author he had protested that "if Lynch is the nominee, I'll be the candidate," meaning that the ties between them were so obvious that the Republican opposition could make political hay by running against "Boss Flynn" rather than battling Lynch's New Deal record in Congress. Flynn yielded, finally, rather than stand in the way of his friend's advancement to the governorship, but his forebodings proved correct.

The next blow came when Impellitteri refused to step aside for Pecora and made it known that if he was not nominated for mayor—the spot he now held temporarily by inheritance—he would run independently. He was fortified in his determination by a direct slap at him by De Sapio.

De Sapio, knowing full well that Pecora was to be the choice, had nevertheless listed six possible mayoral nominees from Manhattan, and Impellitteri's name was last. There were several possible reasons for De Sapio's calculated slur. One was that Impellitteri did not measure up to mayoralty stature, which Impellitteri later proved true. A second lay in the continued sponsorship of Impellitteri by Tommy "Three Finger Brown" Luchese.

While Luchese's role as a reputable businessman remained convincing in most places, the political/underworld grapevine marked him as a man climbing rapidly up the Mafia leadership ladder, to the point of replacing Costello, virtually in retirement, as the underworld's link to big-time politics. Such a development—Luchese's man as mayor—would undercut De Sapio's position as a "reform" leader of Tammany.

The situation developed into one in which De Sapio and Impellitteri became bitter antagonists, personally as well as politically. But the Impellitteri bandwagon gained momentum at a rate which staggered the political community. A whole group of factors, many of which could be viewed as potential liabilities, turned into assets.

First, there was Impellitteri's name, difficult to spell and too long to get into a newspaper headline. The *Daily News* solved this by shortening it to "Impy," and other newspapers rapidly followed suit. It enhanced the pixieish, quixotic appearance of the Impellitteri candidacy—the little man against the bosses. No independent candidate had ever won major office in New York City.

Second, both Pecora, the Democratic nominee, and Edward Corsi, the Republican, were Protestants. The major part of the Italian community, getting a chance to support an Italian for mayor, was predominantly Catholic, and Impellitteri was Catholic.

Third, Governor Dewey, properly discounting the chances of electing a Republican, and eager as always to make the most trouble he could for the Democrats, widely promoted Impellitteri as acting mayor. He conferred with him on city problems, posed with him for pictures, and all but endorsed Impellitteri over Corsi.

Fourth, Pecora, who had won national fame as the tough, unrelenting investigator of Wall Street's pre-Depression fakery and larceny, showed the softening effect of seventeen years on the State Supreme Court bench, and turned out to be a powder-puff campaigner.

Lastly, Impellitteri's smart press secretary, inherited from O'Dwyer, made loud noises from start to finish that "Impy" had spurned a $400,000 bribe from De Sapio to quit the race.

The bribe charge became one of the major issues of the campaign. It was based on the allegation that De Sapio had offered Impellitteri a seat on the State Supreme Court in return for his withdrawal from the mayoralty race. The job paid $28,000, and the term was fourteen years. The $28,000, multiplied by fourteen, amounted to $392,000, leveled off at $400,000 for those who like round numbers.

It is doubtful that De Sapio ever made an offer that could be spelled out that simply. It was against his nature; he preferred indirectness. A group of labor leaders who set up a conference of the two adversaries to see if peace could be negotiated differed afterward on what was said.

Frank Sampson, who was there as Impellitteri's manager, and who also had waterfront labor connections, gave this version:

Mr. De Sapio pleaded with Mr. Impellitteri to withdraw from the race and take a Supreme Court job. When Mr. Impellitteri refused, and said he had refused before, Mr. De Sapio then said: "If you want to remain President of the Council, Vince, I will personally guarantee, and I think I can speak for the other county leaders, you will be nominated for Mayor in three years. How long do you think this man [Pecora] will last? He's sixty-eight or sixty-nine." He then asked Mr. Impellitteri for a few minutes alone. They went into an adjoining room. When they came back, Martin Lacey, as acting chairman [of the labor conferees] asked "What's the verdict?" Mr. Impellitteri said: "I'm still a candidate for Mayor." Mr. Lacey said: "If you're a candidate, I'm 1000% behind you."

The version from Michael J. Quill, head of the Transport Workers Union, was:

Frank Sampson told us he was perfectly willing to instruct Impellitteri to withdraw provided De Sapio would enter into a deal with him on some judgeships and a definite guarantee that Impellitteri would be the Democratic candidate for Mayor in 1953. De Sapio replied that this condition was ridiculous and that he could not commit the Democratic Party to any such deal. He observed no one knew how things would stand in 1953. Quill said he personally asked De Sapio point-blank if a judgeship had been offered to Mr. Impellitteri, and the Tammany leader turned to the Acting Mayor and told him to answer the question. Impellitteri, according to Quill, admitted he never was offered the judgeship. He also admitted that at an earlier meeting at De Sapio's home, he had told the Tammany leader that if any other member of the Board of Estimate was nominated for Mayor, he would support his candidacy. Impellitteri recalled he had told De Sapio, however, that "if there is to be an Italian Mayor of New York, I must be the candidate." Quill said that at this point it was Sampson who suggested a private conference of De Sapio, Impellitteri and Sampson, and when that conference broke up, it was Sampson who said: "There are no commitments here. Vincent will stay in the race."

Both versions alternately ring true and false. De Sapio, in pressing for Impellitteri's withdrawal from the mayoralty race, would have to skirt around Impellitteri's possible future, either as a judge, or as City Council president, the job to which he could revert if the mayor's spot was filled by another. On the other hand, De Sapio was not in a position to promise Impellitteri the mayoralty three years ahead, and it was not his habit to make such offers so far in advance. As things worked out, it did not matter who was telling how much of the truth. The public, always willing to believe in stories of deals by bosses, accepted the version of the Impellitteri camp that a "bribe" had been offered and spurned.

Ed Flynn's carefully conceived plan for a big Democratic mayoralty vote that would help elect a Democratic governor worked in reverse. The Democrats split down the middle on the mayoralty, and the split wreaked havoc on the party vote for governor and U.S. senator. Dewey was easily elected over Lynch for a third four-year term as governor. Herbert Lehman won his full-term Senate seat by a small margin, and that only because an internal quarrel among the Republicans put their nominee, Joe Hanley, at odds with the governor. Pecora got only 935,000 votes for mayor; Corsi, who had the courage to raise Impellitteri's connections with Luchese as a campaign issue, got the Republican minimum, 382,000. Impellitteri, running alone and cast as the heroic independent, got 1,161,000, making him temporarily the biggest man in town. He was now mayor in his own right and would be for the next three years. Could De Sapio survive as leader of Tammany? Could he hold his votes in the executive committee against the inevitable pressure from a Tammany-oriented mayor who had reason to regard De Sapio as hostile?

There were many in the executive committee who did not think so. During the campaign itself, Sampson, still a district leader, had been joined by Bob Blaikie, a perpetual West Side insurgent, in publicly backing Impellitteri's candidacy, and quiet support had come from Harry Brickman and several others who had been gravitating to the Luchese power center. Then, right after election, almost as soon as the votes had been counted, "the Indian," Mancuso, let it be known he was joining the rebels.

In his case, retribution from Costello came fast.

The election-district captains in Mancuso's Harlem bailiwick met in the home of one of them, and at the meeting's conclusion signed a round-robin declaring that Mancuso was no longer the district leader. This would have caused no furor or public lament if the district captains had met voluntarily. But the pro-Impy forces quickly leaked the fact that there had been two underworld representatives present, wielding the whip for De Sapio and reform.

They were identified as Joey Rao and Joe Stracci, also known as Joe Stretch. Rao, with a record of sixteen arrests and many convictions, was still under bond as a suspect in the Scottoriggio killing of 1946. Joe Stretch's record was similar. At the Harlem session, they issued the orders and the captains issued their disclaimer of Mancuso. District Attorney Hogan, opening a grand-jury investigation of the affair, said: "The presence of Rao and Stracci had the same effect as if they had leveled a gun at the heads of the captains."

De Sapio, summoned as a witness before the grand jury, willingly waived immunity. He told the investigators, and afterward the press, that he had been at the meeting, been introduced to everyone there, and had shaken hands all around, but that the group, while he was there, did not include Rao and Stracci. "If I had known they were going to be there, I would not have gone," he said.

There is no reason to question De Sapio's statement that he and the gunmen were not in the room at the same time. The fact could have been checked out in the course of the questioning of everyone else. The press never made the connection between Mancuso's ouster and De Sapio's future as leader of Tammany. But no one on the inside of politics questioned what it added up to, which was that Costello's troops, though dwindling in number, could still go to De Sapio's assistance if it looked as if he needed help.

De Sapio's official comment on Impellitteri's mayoral victory was restrained and dignified: "The people of New York County can be assured that their welfare will always have the first consideration from the Democratic Party. This will be our guide in supporting Mayor Impellitteri. Our aim is cooperation, not negation."

In his capacity as a member of the Board of Elections, De Sapio signed Impellitteri's certificate of election as mayor. He did not go across the street to City Hall to the party marking the swearing in of his opponent. He had not been invited.

SIX

HANGING IN THE BALANCE

Vincent Impellitteri was fifty years old when he was elected New York City's 101st mayor. For a quarter-century he had practiced law and politicked as a lower-echelon Tammany spear carrier. The highest reward the organization ever had given him was a secretary-ship to a State Supreme Court justice. He was plucked from this obscurity and made president of the City Council, the municipal equivalent of the federal vice-presidency. This, as previously noted, was the result of the efforts of Luchese, the Mafia big shot, but the people did not know this, and neither did most politicians.

As City Council president for four years and seven months of O'Dwyer's mayoralty, Impellitteri proved the perfect Throttlebot-tom. He voted as the mayor told him to, on matters he did not neces-sarily understand, and spent most of his waking hours shaking hands at public dinners, political clambakes, and cornerstone layings too unimportant to merit the mayor's presence.

So the scope of his campaign for mayor in 1950 surprised the professional politicians who knew him, and they attributed its suc-cess, with reason, to his imaginative press secretary, Bill Donoghue. No matter who was responsible, Impellitteri's role as an independent, anti-boss candidate who would lead the city in new directions was brilliantly conceived and acted out. In an early coup, he bought the support of Robert Moses by privately promising Moses an even freer hand than he had had in the planning and carrying out of park, high-way, and housing projects. Moses was then at the peak of his prestige as the city's master builder. Impellitteri scored more heavily still when he appointed Thomas F. Murphy as police commissioner to succeed an O'Dwyer holdover.

Murphy, as a federal prosecutor, had just convicted Alger Hiss where other men had failed, and his presence in the Impellitteri camp bestowed the valuable cachet of anti-Communism on the Impellitteri campaign in that opening year of Senator Joe McCarthy's reign of terror. All that Impellitteri's chief rival, Pecora, could do was to pledge to retain Murphy if he were elected.

The relationship that existed between Luchese, the mayor, and the new police commissioner is one that still puzzles the author. State Crime Commission hearings in 1952 brought out testimony that Luchese had rushed to Murphy's home to congratulate him personally the night his appointment as the police head was announced. What has never been printed is the report that during the Impellitteri administration Luchese, Impellitteri, and Murphy met regularly for lunch, once a week, in an Italian restaurant halfway between Police Headquarters and City Hall. On the one hand, it is impossible to believe that the mayor and the police commissioner knew they were lunching publicly with the Mafia chieftain known as Three Finger Brown. On the other hand, it is difficult to comprehend that the police commissioner of New York did not know who headed the Mafia.

However, these were developments of which the public knew nothing. What did become clear almost immediately was what kind of a mayor Impellitteri intended to be.

Impellitteri did not intend to transform himself into a tireless genius conceiving great ideas for the city. He just wanted a comfortable term as an easy-going mayor who could get himself reelected—with the support of the party machines—when the next mayoralty election was held. Later on, he seemed to close the door of his private office to keep out the problems, leaving policy-making in the hands of Moses and the city's Bureau of the Budget.

In his first week in office he let down with a dull thud the people who expected things of him as a political reformer and an independent. His first major appointment was of Frank Sampson as his "patronage secretary," and this former leader of Tammany Hall got the headlines while the new mayor vacationed in Havana. The appointment struck a sour note for those who did not rank job patronage high on the mayor's priority list. Impellitteri made it just as clear, just as fast, that he considered his only enemy to be De Sapio. This had the effect of turning what might have been a crusade against political machines into a personal vendetta, and as such it got no support from the press or the public. The lack of that support proved important in saving for De Sapio his Tammany leadership and his political career.

There had to be other things working in De Sapio's favor, however, and there were. During the fifteen months he had been Tammany boss he had strengthened himself with individual district leaders, particularly among the Irish bloc of the West Side. He won the confidence and respect of many in that group who had never felt comfortable with any of the previous Tammany bosses who had sprung from Costello roots, even if they were Irish themselves, like Kennedy and Loughlin. The West Siders, steeped in Tammany tradition, preferred to deal with a boss who spoke as the boss and who worked out organization problems without waiting to be told what to do. They had been brought up in politics on the principle of loyalty to the leader, and they had longed for a leader worthy of the name. Before De Sapio's advent they had formed the natural nucleus of any opposition to the so-called leadership they had endured, a leadership foreign to their tradition. De Sapio had proved himself a leader, and in his first crisis most of them stood with him.

Impellitteri's first move against De Sapio was an attempt to downgrade him and hit him in his pocketbook by denying him renomination to the Board of Elections. The Irish bloc joined the Costello men in resenting it. Dennis J. Mahon, senior statesman of the West Siders, looked around the room at the executive committee members who had gone along with De Sapio in backing Pecora over Impellitteri, and said: "If guessing wrong on mayor makes a man unfit, every man in this room is guilty."

He spoke confidently and accurately, because Sampson, Blaikie, and the identifiable members of the Luchese clique then, and later, showed their dissent by staying away from executive committee meetings. De Sapio followed up his show of executive committee support by a propaganda coup: he wrote to each of the 11,985 members of the county committee, asking their support for the Board of Elections post. Under the law the county committeemen did the actual voting on that job, but in the past they had been treated as stooges who would do what their district leaders told them to do. The maneuver made De Sapio appear the proponent of political democracy and the opposition as boss-ridden traditionalists. De Sapio won the Election Board skirmish with ease, and Impellitteri never launched the full-scale attack on De Sapio's Tammany leadership which he had planned. Sampson, who might have pushed for moves in that direction, seemed to prefer being the mayor's sole patronage dispenser rather than share the privilege with someone he might install in the Tammany leadership. In any event, from then on there were only scattered brush fires. The mayor would detach a De Sapio follower from the public payroll; De Sapio's forces would win a district primary fight; Luchese would quietly detach a follower from Costello; all without a change in the balance of power.

The really calculated assistance De Sapio received in the three years of the Impellitteri administration came from Ed Flynn, who was Democratic national committeeman from New York as well as Bronx boss, and the nearest thing to a state boss that the party had. Happy-go-lucky and active, although his doctors had warned him that his heart would give him no further notice before it stopped beating, Flynn considered De Sapio a friend as well as a colleague who relieved him of much drudgery and legwork. Loyalty to De Sapio was more important to Flynn than any job patronage Impellitteri could have withheld from the Bronx in reprisal, had he dared.

So Flynn was De Sapio's federal angel. The patronage-rich offices of Collector of Internal Revenue, United States Attorney, Postmaster of New York, Director of the Office of Price Stabilization, and many others were filled with men bearing De Sapio's political brand. And they were men who reflected no discredit on their sponsor.

The court system, Tammany's old patronage standby, also remained loyal to De Sapio, and with reason. He never sent a note to a judge telling him whom to appoint. He conferred with the judge and let him choose among nominees. More important, he made drastic alterations in the old system of selling judicial nominations.

Tammany sold judgeships throughout its history. Sometimes the sales could be rationalized on the basis of campaign contributions made to the party over a long period of time by a wealthy family, the same way some men have won ambassadorships to desirable foreign capitals. More frequently they just reflected the will of the party leaders at the moment to take cash and let the credit go. The amazing facts, nevertheless, are: that no *elective* judge who paid for his nomination has ever been proven to have done so, in a court of law or via any investigation, although a number of *appointive* judges have been convicted of paying; and that no elective judge who paid for his nomination has gotten into provable difficulties because he was found to have exercised less than impartial justice.

A probably apocryphal story about an elective judge is a Tammany chestnut which runs as follows: A leader, attempting to "fix" a case, went to the judge trying it. The judge refused to take the necessary steps. The leader told the judge, "You owe it to me and the organization." The judge replied, "I don't owe anybody a damn thing. I paid cash on the barrelhead."

But while the public knew little of the facts of judicial sales, the bar associations knew, and so did individual attorneys, who either felt it demeaned them as well as justice to participate in buying a place on the bench, or else could not raise the $75,000 needed.

In the De Sapio regime the price was cut drastically. A nominee to the bench paid roughly the equivalent of one year's salary of the court post involved, and was told the money went for campaign expenses. This had the dual effect of saving the purchaser a considerable amount of cash and giving him a basis for convincing himself that he had not bought his seat but had simply contributed to his party.

Another refinement of the system under De Sapio won almost unanimous approval of the lower-court judges, since it gave them the hope of promotion. As De Sapio worked it out, if a vacancy occurred on the State Supreme Court—the highest court of original jurisdiction —a judge from the next-ranking City Court was named to fill it; a

Municipal Court judge was named to the City Court vacancy thus created, and some assemblyman or state senator was named to the newly opened Municipal Court post. Each paid a price roughly equivalent to one year's difference in the salary. In addition, there were more bench nominations awarded for purely party service, without payment of cash, than there had been in the years immediately preceding De Sapio's advent.

The new approach did not satisfy the stiff-necked Bar Association, which continued to campaign for a purely appointive judiciary to which it would make the original nominations, but illegal as it was, the De Sapio system was very satisfactory to the Tammany organization and to the courts, which gave De Sapio continued political support during his battle with Impellitteri.

The spring of 1951 was a rough season for De Sapio, as well as nearly everyone else connected with New York politics, regardless of party or faction. The Senate committee investigating organized crime, headed by Senator Estes Kefauver of Tennessee, was holding public hearings all over the nation. In New York the committee concentrated on links between the underworld and politics. And the hearings were televised. Every afternoon for a week, the Kefauver hearings stopped the clock in every bar and grill and living room that housed a television set.

The concocted story that Mayor Impellitteri had first been chosen for City Council president as the result of a thumbing through of the Little Green Book fascinated the public. It gasped at the testimony of John P. Crane, president of the Uniformed Firemen's Association, that he had given $55,000 to O'Dwyer's Jim Moran, and $10,000 to Mayor O'Dwyer himself, on the porch of Gracie Mansion. It listened uncomprehendingly to O'Dwyer's attempts to explain Police Department corruption, in which O'Dwyer's own close friends had figured, and how it happened that Abe Reles, the key witness in the Anastasia murder case while O'Dwyer was district attorney, had died while in the custody of O'Dwyer's hand-picked cops. And how O'Dwyer knew Costello only as a result of his attempt to straighten out labor troubles at Wright Field. It learned that Governor Dewey, whom it had always regarded as a crusader for reform, had let professional gamblers operate the wide-open casinos at the Saratoga spa upstate, and also that the governor refused to come down to New York and testify, or, in fact, testify even if the committee came to him.

The Kefauver hearings smeared the reputations of so many in politics that neither major party gained or suffered particularly. The hearings did serve to make the senator himself a frontrunner for the 1952 Democratic presidential nomination, and locally, the publicity elected the committee's counsel, Rudolph Halley, as president of the City Council in the 1951 election held to fill the vacancy in that post caused by the promotion of Impellitteri to mayor. The victory of Halley, running on the Liberal Party ticket against separate Democratic and Republican nominees, provided the first proof of the power of television as a political tool. Until he appeared on its screen, nobody in New York politics had ever heard of Halley.

Costello's testimony made a principal dent, possibly because he was the first "name" witness and also because the thread of Costello connections ran through the testimony of so many others. As the names of individual Tammany district leaders were read off, Costello admitted knowing them, and with a careless ease the former bootlegger and gambler admitted that he knew a lot of people who could help others and that the district leaders had frequently come to him for the kind of assistance his friends could render.

His connection with the Aurelio case was rehashed, and for the first time it was disclosed that he had been helpful in promoting the careers of men serving on the bench in Queens. One of them was a Republican. But this was more or less overlooked in the light of the repeated connection of Costello with De Sapio and the leaders who made up a majority of the Tammany executive committee.

In this, the hearings were recounting history rather than reflecting the situation actually current in Tammany. Luchese had moved slowly ahead in the friendly atmosphere of the Impellitteri administration and at the time of the Kefauver hearings would have been a more realistic target than Costello, who was in retirement, at least to the extent that investigating bodies permitted him to relax. There was not a single mention of Luchese in the Kefauver probe.

It was not until the following year, when a state crime commis-

sion held hearings—not televised—that Luchese was publicly identified as Costello's successor as leader of the Mafia. There was this
comment in the final report from the commission: "Luchese led a
unique kind of double life."

De Sapio reacted vigorously to the Kefauver testimony. He challenged the Bar Association to investigate every one of Tammany's
nominees for judicial office since he had become leader to determine
whether Costello could make judges or still had influence in Tammany.

He had told the Kefauver Committee under oath: "Costello is
not a power in Tammany Hall, not a power behind Tammany Hall.
He does not dictate nominations. He does not control, nor has he any
influence over my policies or those of the Democratic organization in
this county in any way, shape or form."

He amplified this to the Bar Association, saying: "I am trying to
be realistic about it. I know that if I got on top of the Empire State
Building and shouted from now to doomsday, or if I went to some
holy place and took an oath that it was untrue, the result would be
the same. Nothing would be accomplished in the way of convincing
the man in the street. So instead of mere words, I have taken action.
Maybe you will think this action is unusual for Tammany Hall and
a Tammany leader, but these are unusual times and the challenge
to me I recognize as unusual."

After spelling out his challenge to the Bar Association, he recalled outstanding jurists, such as Federal Court judge Edward Weinfeld, a Lehman protégé, and Supreme Court justice Charles D.
Breitel, a Dewey protégé, both seated on the bench during De Sapio's
period of leadership. The Bar Association did not accept De Sapio's
challenge. If it had, he would have stood on safe ground, for not one
of the dozen or more judges of high courts who owed their places to
De Sapio had any underworld connections or sponsorship.

De Sapio criticized the Kefauver investigators for making no
distinction in the varying degrees of intimacy existing between Costello and Tammany district leaders, saying: "If the answers had been
accurate ones, the result would have been a Tammany whitewash.
We were convicted of guilt by association and conjecture."

De Sapio was too good a political field-general to content himself with remaining on the defensive. So while he jabbed back at the professional Tammany tormenters, he continued his long-range offensive of identifying Tammany with the popular side of public issues and himself as the enlightened leader of political machinery that operated for the public good.

Unlike any of his predecessors, whose orders to kill or support pending legislation in Albany or the City Council were always confined to passing the word privately, De Sapio played his role publicly, and missed no opportunity to appear on the progressive and liberal side. Stanley Lowell, as the assistant to Borough President Wagner specializing in the field of social reforms, once mentioned to De Sapio that Tammany should support President Truman's Fair Employment Practices legislation, a Magna Carta for the black community which was being blocked in Congress by a Republican-Dixiecrat coalition

De Sapio telephoned every New York congressman and issued, in their and the party's behalf, a statement backing the Truman bill. He made a regular habit of conferring with the party's legislative leaders in Albany and the City Council, giving party backing in his own name to one bill here, fighting another there. When *The New York Times* inquired editorially what business party leaders had conferring on legislation, De Sapio wrote back to the *Times,* "It is because the party leaders are in touch with the people and aware of their wishes. We have not the right to forfeit the responsibility."

He took the lead in opposing a projected Dewey-Impellitteri increase in the city sales tax from 2 to 3 percent. He fought the similarly sponsored legislation creating the Transit Authority, which carried with it an increase in the subway and bus fares from ten cents to fifteen. He predicted that under the Transit Authority concept the fare would eventually rise to twenty-five cents. (They went to thirty cents in 1970.)

He promulgated legislative programs as though he were an elected officeholder, calling for better housing legislation, for continued rent control, for compulsory automobile and health insurance, for permanent registration of voters, for voting for eighteen-year-olds, for the use of voting machines in primary elections. He urged that party officials who used the protection of the Fifth Amendment, barring self-incrimination, forfeit their party posts.

He supported the broadening of existing programs for day-care centers and recreational facilities for both youth and the aging. Inevitably, he was drawn into closer contact with the social reformers in the city's informal establishment. Settlement-house heads such as Helen Hall of the Henry Street Settlement came to trust him and to work with him. So did Frank Karelson of the Public Education Association, whom De Sapio supported in the unending battle for more money for the school system.

As Impellitteri's term drew toward its end and a new mayoralty election approached, De Sapio increased the pace of his activity in the social welfare field. He set up a rent-information office for tenement dwellers, under the supervision of a Tammany corps of young lawyers. He circulated petitions against the 15 percent rent-increase bill being enacted by the legislature and got 200,000 protest signatures.

To demonstrate again that Tammany Hall was a democratic institution, and imply that his opposition to Mayor Impellitteri was not personal, he sent out postcards to 41,000 — a 10 percent random selection of the enrolled Democrats in New York County, asking the single question: "Do you want Vincent Impellitteri as your candidate for mayor?" The response was four to one in the negative.

He worked closely with Borough President Wagner, who had already decided that association with the Impellitteri administration was a kiss of political death and was formulating, with De Sapio's encouragement, a city-wide program of his own. De Sapio suggested positions Wagner's office might take and prompted him to act on the popular side of an issue before Rudolph Halley, whom De Sapio recognized as a mayoral threat for 1953, could preempt it.

In the same spirit that De Sapio collected issues on which his party would look good, so did he collect a stable of potential nominees for high office, and he groomed them as carefully as a racetrack trainer would handle Derby hopefuls.

Chronologically, the first of these was Wagner. But De Sapio also developed a warm relationship with District Attorney Hogan, whose record of scrupulous nonpartisan administration of his DA's office made him a figure who could be trotted out for any higher office at the propitious moment.

Then he adopted Averell Harriman. This distinguished expert in foreign policy, who had served as diplomatic troubleshooter for both Franklin D. Roosevelt and Harry Truman, was a multimillionaire New Yorker who was unhappy being out of government. Flynn and De Sapio picked Harriman as New York's favorite-son candidate for the Democratic presidential nomination in 1952. For a period the backing of President Truman gave Harriman's run some needed national support. At the Chicago convention Truman switched back to Adlai Stevenson of Illinois, who had been his original choice. At the right moment, New York switched its ninety votes from Harriman to Stevenson, putting Stevenson over the top for the nomination.

De Sapio and Harriman established a close friendship thereafter. Harriman was never a possibility for mayor, since all his many residences were outside the city, but he was a substantial financial contributor, and with his reputation could be groomed for governor or senator.

Flynn was frequently out of the city, representing his law firm in Washington or taking some of the precious days left of his life to vacation at his horse-breeding farm in Kentucky. He encouraged rather than resented De Sapio's long-range political aims and planning.

The last horse in the De Sapio stable was young Franklin D. Roosevelt, who had been reelected to Congress, with Tammany's support rather than its opposition, in 1950 and in 1952. Although Roosevelt at one time had endorsed a move by Bob Blaikie to oust De Sapio as Tammany leader in favor of Blaikie himself, De Sapio publicly forgave and forgot. He put Roosevelt on the Tammany list of officially sponsored delegates to the 1952 convention and kept him on his reserve list of potential candidates for higher office.

De Sapio had seized two main municipal issues on which he could run a candidate for mayor in 1953, as well as two possible candidates to carry the De Sapio banner against Impellitteri in the Democratic primary, since the mayor had clearly indicated his intention of seeking the Democratic nomination for a second term. The issues were responsibility for the fifteen-cent subway and bus fares and for the blanket 15 percent increase in controlled rents. Both were easy to lay at Impellitteri's door, although they had been adopted by the legislature at Dewey's request. Impellitteri, and O'Dwyer before him, had an understanding with the governor that in return for Dewey's helping them on minor city problems or partisan affairs, they would accept his state policies without too much fuss.

De Sapio, scanning the list of possible opponents for Impellitteri, decided that Hogan and Wagner were the most hopeful prospects, offering both respectability and the promise of victory. He checked first with Hogan. Without committing himself to Hogan's support, he wanted to know if Hogan was interested. The district attorney made it clear that while he was interested in becoming mayor, he would not run a campaign based on the rent and fare issues, because this would involve attacking Governor Dewey, his original boss and political sponsor. In fact, Hogan indicated, he preferred to run, if he ran at all, as the joint nominee of the Republican and Democratic parties, as he had always done for the district attorneyship. From De Sapio's point of view, this eliminated Hogan as a candidate for mayor in 1953, and he turned to Wagner.

Wagner was not yet a candidate. He and his staff, including the author, had decided late in 1952 that the concentration for the following six months had to be on building up a positive record of accomplishment in office; that while the purpose of this was political in the broadest sense of the word, there should be no political discussions as such, lest politics creep into the governmental activities. Wagner's programs were expanded to the point that he was running, in effect, a small-scale administration rival to Impellitteri's. The effect was to insulate Wagner from the mayor, but any discussion of a possible mayoralty race by the borough president was taboo.

De Sapio broached the subject of a Wagner candidacy to the author in April 1953. Typically, the meeting took place in a taxicab. De Sapio always favored the taxicab as a conference room. It assured him maximum privacy—if the window between driver and passenger was kept closed—and it was also a time saver for a man who kept so

demanding a schedule that he was always late for the next appointment. While riding from the City Hall area to the Biltmore, the conversation went as follows:

"Warren, what is Bob's thinking?"

"About what, the mayoralty?"

"Yes."

The author explained the office taboo on political discussions
and that he therefore could not speak for Wagner. But he could express his own judgment as to what Wagner would do.

"Given the support of two counties, Manhattan and the Bronx..."

"I wouldn't ask him to go in with only one," interjected De Sapio.

"Well, given two counties and independent support, like Eleanor
Roosevelt and Herbert Lehman, I think he'd make the race."

"Thanks, that's what I wanted to know," said De Sapio.

But the author pursued it further. "Who's your candidate," he
asked.

"Well," said De Sapio, "you know that when I sit down with Ed
Flynn, I always listen to him and get his ideas first."

"Yes, but suppose the Bronx has no candidate. How many candidates do you have from Manhattan?"

"One," said De Sapio.

"Who?"

"Wagner," was the immediate answer.

"Thanks," said the author. "That is what I wanted to know."

The exchange served De Sapio's purpose well. Without a face-
to-face exchange he had found out the circumstances under which
Wagner would run, had expressed his own view, but had avoided a
formal commitment. The hedge was that unless both he and Flynn
agreed on Wagner, the nomination would go elsewhere.

The author never repeated the conversation to Wagner, and
Wagner and De Sapio never discussed it. Both were too cagy, and
preferred to await developments rather than talk in advance.

Eventually De Sapio and Flynn together canvassed the field and
agreed on Wagner as their nominee. He was to carry the banner of
New York and Bronx counties against the other three, just as Jimmy
Walker had been entered in the primary against another bumbling

mayor, John F. Hylan, a quarter-century earlier. Roe's leadership in Queens and Sullivan's in Richmond had long since yielded to Impellitteri's patronage persuasions; they backed the mayor. Kenneth Sutherland, the Brooklyn boss, first leaned to Wagner, but Luchese's influence, strong with Sutherland, finally placed him in Impellitteri's corner.

There was a revealing incident one noon early in the spring of 1953 at the Yale Club, Wagner's favorite spot for private conferences. That day the conferees, discussing some nonmayoral problems, were Wagner, the author, then commissioner of borough works, and De Sapio. With De Sapio absent from the table for a few moments making a telephone call, Wagner remarked to his aide: "I hear Carmine is seeing the Halley people. I wonder how much substance there is to it."

Later, when Wagner was at the checkroom collecting his hat, the author asked De Sapio whether he was negotiating with Halley, the Kefauver Committee crusader, about a possible Tammany endorsement for mayor. De Sapio's reply was: "That's a laugh. He sent word to me that he might have to kick me around a bit during the campaign, but that things would be all right after election. Can you imagine? If the people can't trust him, how could I?"

SEVEN

VICTORY

The 1953 alliance of De Sapio and Wagner, solemnized when Carmine embraced Bob as his man for mayor, turned into the most successful marriage of boss and candidate that New York politics had seen. The nearest thing to it had been the working relationship of Governor Al Smith and Charles F. Murphy thirty years earlier.

The De Sapio–Wagner partnership probably was so successful because it proved so mutually rewarding. Once each had adapted to it, neither had any incentive to break it up. It led to the election and reelection of Wagner as mayor and gave him statewide recognition as the party's most reliable vote getter. It made De Sapio the boss of his party in the city, then in the state and, as national committeeman, its spokesman in national politics. It gave Wagner the completely reliable political agent that a successful administration must have; it gave De Sapio all the scope he could want as a political leader and as the seeker of a clean new countenance for all political leadership.

Its fringe benefits, which affected the party more directly than they did the participating pair, included:

1. The establishment of the liberal wing of the Democratic Party as its controlling element, with De Sapio as its willing majordomo.

2. The long-delayed reform of Tammany's system of electing its boss and its district leaders, and the complete erosion of underworld influence.

3. The unseating of a number of conservative-minded old-line party bosses in the city and on Long Island, most notably in Queens, Richmond, Nassau, and Suffolk counties.

4. The recapture by the Democrats of the governorship, which the party had not held since Herbert Lehman voluntarily relinquished that office back in 1942.

Up to 1953 Wagner and De Sapio had not been close. Even after De Sapio had turned to Wagner for the borough presidency in 1949, the two had dealt at arm's length, De Sapio never pressing for, and Wagner never offering more than the circumstance of the moment demanded. Then their work together as the underdogs in the 1953 primary campaign for mayor cemented their relationship. The primary was an intimate, shirt-sleeve operation on the part of a handful of men learning to work as a team. Its smooth progression toward success bound all the participants together then and for many years thereafter.

The campaign was one of the cheapest on record, financed on a shoestring. Big money did not come in until after the primary. Even at 1953 prices, the $130,000 that was spent was small change for a city-wide effort. The campaign manager, Adrian Burke, later to be rewarded for his efforts by appointment as Wagner's corporation counsel and then election to the state's highest court, had been chosen in desperation after the other possibilities on a long list proved too busy or uninterested. Burke turned out to be a twenty-four-hour-a-day operator, alternately a conciliator of differences among others and an inspired commander on his own. De Sapio appeared here, there, and everywhere, invariably coming up with a means toward any desired end. Wagner's small staff in the borough president's office served effectively, each member in his specialty, and Wagner himself contributed sagely and unassumingly to a smooth, smart operation.

It was De Sapio who conducted negotiations to make up the balance of the Wagner ticket. Lawrence Gerosa emerged as the candidate of the Flynn machine for the controllership and was accepted without question. There was practical necessity to find a Brooklyn man, with a following of his own, to run for the City Council presidency, and De Sapio's recommendation of Abe Stark was accepted.

To succeed Wagner as borough president, the politics of the day called for a black man, since the Republican and Liberal parties were already fielding black candidates for the general election. Men such as Ralph Bunche and A. Philip Randolph were approached, and they declined. As the deadline neared, De Sapio said: "We've explored the stratosphere, and gotten no place. We have to get down to the practical, political level. On that level we have Adam Powell, Earl Brown and Hulan Jack. Adam is too controversial, Brown does well at the district level, but might not at the borough level. What's the matter with Hulan Jack?"

At the time, there was nothing the matter with him, and the Jack nomination was accepted by Wagner and his advisers. Jack was then a respected assemblyman from Harlem.

When it came to the campaign itself, Wagner had too much political savoir-faire to think that a candidate can manage his own campaign as well as wage it, a mistake often made by less astute and less successful office seekers. He would sit in on the strategy sessions and say his piece, or just listen. The thinking of De Sapio, or Burke, or lesser campaign aides such as the author was as likely to be adopted as that of the candidate himself. Once policy had been decided, Wagner left the details and implementation to those who were not tied down, as he was, to a schedule of morning-to-midnight campaign speeches and appearances.

While Wagner was viewed as the outsider in the race—and his public relations staff carefully preserved that role for him as long as possible—the betting odds that made Impellitteri a sure winner were wrong from the start. The race, like so many others, was decided in advance by the issues, records, and personalities of the men involved. It was true that Impellitteri had the backing of the Democratic organizations in Brooklyn, Queens, and Richmond, while Wagner had solid support from the machine only in the Bronx. In Manhattan, with Costello in retirement—and in or out of federal prison, depending on the legal writ of the moment—Luchese's henchmen had inched close to control. De Sapio could count on a bare 50 percent of the votes in the Tammany executive committee in support of Wagner. It was also true that Impellitteri, as the incumbent, had contributors whose ample funds were his to spend, and he had the machinery of the whole city administration to operate in his behalf.

But there is that old political rule of thumb that a candidate with an issue to attract the public, and with part of the machine behind him, can beat the rest of the organization in a primary. Wagner did not merely have one issue, he had all of them—the rent, tax, and fare increases to which Impellitteri had been a party, plus continued overcrowding in the schools. To supplement Wagner's share of the party regulars there were hordes of volunteers, a much rarer manifestation of political support then than now. The parent-teacher organizations, with strength in every borough, had become impressed with Wagner's stance on education, demonstrated by his votes in the Board of Estimate. Their individual groups mobilized as an underground army to do battle for Wagner, and their ranks were swelled by the best-organized unions within the CIO, notably Mike Quill's Transport Workers Union. For a last-minute pre-primary mailing of Wagner literature, no fewer than five hundred of these volunteers stood all night in the corridors of the headquarters hotel, addressing and stuffing endless rows of envelopes on the long wooden counters which served as desks. It was an impressive display.

On primary day itself the eager, unpaid Wagner workers outmanned, outmaneuvered, and outfought the opposition from the moth-eaten organizations in getting out the vote and in seeing that it was counted honestly. The result was not even close; Wagner got 350,484 votes and Impellitteri 181,295. Wagner had drawn the first position on the ballot, so his slogan "Vote Row A All the Way" swept in his entire ticket in every borough but Richmond, where, although central Wagner headquarters had not even tried, the local Wagner supporters came within an eyelash of victory.

The New York Times, which up to primary night had taken an equally dim view of both Wagner and Impellitteri, hailed Wagner's victory as one that put the liberal wing of the party in control. More important, the leading lights among the liberals came to the same conclusion simultaneously and independently. At headquarters the telephone switchboard was deluged with calls, from Adlai Stevenson in Illinois; Harry S. Truman in Independence, Missouri; Eleanor Roosevelt in Hyde Park; Herbert Lehman in Washington; and many, many others of the same political stripe all over the country. The messages were joyous and excited as they hailed the results.

To the callers it was not the borough president who had won, but the old New Deal, and in New York, its birthplace. Wagner's victory gave them hope of a comeback nationally for their philosophy of government. They had long lacked even grounds for such hope: Stevenson had been slaughtered running for President the previous year, the old Republican-Dixiecrat alliance was running the House of Representatives, and the Senate was jumping to the crack of Joe McCarthy's bullwhip.

Truman and Stevenson already had a slight acquaintance with De Sapio. Truman, party regular that he was, had chosen the year before to speak in New York under De Sapio's aegis rather than Impellitteri's. De Sapio had set up a separate Manhattan For Stevenson headquarters, to demonstrate Tammany's loyalty to even a sure loser. However, most of those of the Roosevelt-Truman era who called Wagner's exuberant headquarters that night had dealt in the past with Ed Flynn. But Flynn had died in the spring, shortly after giving Wagner his political blessing as the man to beat Impellitteri, so this night the national figures in the party talked to De Sapio and identified him as one of their own. It was the beginning of status for De Sapio as a national party leader.

The national leaders no longer had to worry about underworld influence in the Tammany that De Sapio led. The Wagner slate in the primary had been complete down to nominees for county-committee membership, who in turn elected district leaders. Twelve incumbent Tammany district leaders had openly defected to Impellitteri during the campaign, and others had done so covertly. But the pro-Wagner slates, put on the ballot by De Sapio's efforts, carried every one of the sixteen assembly districts.

The sweep resulted in the defeat of every leader identified with Luchese's mob. It was the greatest purge in Tammany's long history. Their successors, in alliance with those who had never had under-

115

world ties, made control of the Tammany executive committee no longer dependent even on Costello's benevolence. De Sapio now had a majority in his own right.

The November election campaign turned out to be as simple and successful as the primary had been. Impellitteri made noises about running as an independent; but his money men went over to Wagner and that ended that. Halley's campaign as an anti-boss independent Democrat running on the Liberal Party line was thrown off stride by—and never recovered from—the revelation that Halley had secretly sought De Sapio's support for the Democratic nomination. After the disclosure, made by Wagner in a speech, Halley mulled over his reply for a full five days and then issued a flat denial that he had ever done anything of the kind. De Sapio produced the go-between, who confirmed the original charge, and then Carmine rubbed salt in Halley's wounds by adding, "He and his friends did everything possible to assure the very people he now denounces as bosses that he would serve them faithfully and well."

The Wagner–De Sapio strategy was to dismiss Halley as a hypocritical "spoiler" whose only effect on the campaign might be to elect the Republican nominee, Harold Riegelman, identified with the city's real estate interests, and to run against Riegelman as if he were the real opposition. They bombarded Riegelman with the same salvos that had sunk Impellitteri—the rent, fare, and tax increases of the previous spring. The strategy was completely successful. The election results were: Wagner 1,022,626, Riegelman 661,591, and Halley 467,105. Wagner carried every borough but Queens, where Riegelman emerged with a margin of fewer than 1,000 votes.

At a stage of the campaign when it was apparent that the election was in the bag, Wagner surprised even some of his own campaign aides by coming out for the creation of the post of city administrator in the mayor's office. Wagner had previously opposed the concept as an unnecessary step toward the city-manager form of government. Behind the switch in Wagner's position was a revealing glimpse of things to come in the political and governmental operations of the Wagner–De Sapio team.

The idea of a city administrator who would supervise municipal operations—as distinct from policies—to make them more efficient had been urged by a governmental study group known as the Mayor's Committee on Management Survey, which had been set up in the last year of the O'Dwyer administration, but which made its final report in the last year of Impellitteri's. The group, headed by the eminent Luther Gulick of the Institute of Public Administration, estimated that a city administrator could save the city $75 million a year in operating expenses, a sum worth talking about in a pre-inflation economy.

Wagner and De Sapio agreed that the newspaper editorial writers would hang the report around the neck of a new city administration unless they did something about it. They decided to sound out Gulick. Would he take the job of city administrator himself? If so, Wagner would pledge himself to create it. Gulick said yes privately, and then Wagner came out publicly for the creation of the new post.

The thinking was simple. Neither Wagner nor De Sapio believed anyone could cut city spending by $75 million, for what might be saved in one area would always be needed in another. But letting Gulick carry the ball for efficiency would be a definite plus, no matter what the final fiscal results, for if he could not save that amount it would be proof that no one could, and if he managed the miracle the administration would get the credit. Either way, it would take the heat off the new administration. De Sapio's intimate participation in the Gulick coup was an early manifestation of the meshing of political tactics and governmental programing which was to mark the first two Wagner administrations.

It produced later an incident which amused the few who learned of it. Early in the Wagner administration Gulick became involved in a power struggle with Budget Director Abe Beame for control of the city's Division of Research and Analysis, then a part of the Budget Bureau. Gulick wanted it in his office. Wagner temporized on deciding between the claims of two principal lieutenants and faithful aides. At a luncheon for a foreign dignitary, where several of the speeches were in an incomprehensible tongue, Gulick found himself seated next to De Sapio and took advantage of the proximity to whisper to him an appeal for political support.

When Wagner heard of this venture in pressure politics by the apolitical Gulick, he exploded as he always did when a subordinate tried to cut a corner. Wagner was expert at delegating administrative detail, but he never delegated policy making. He wanted to be in at the start of a problem and to hear the outcome later, as well as the plan of action that had been followed. Anyone who tried to influence his decision without his knowledge was in for trouble. In this case he did not blame De Sapio. He merely held up Gulick's acquisition of the Bureau of Research and Analysis for an additional six months, to teach him who was boss.

De Sapio himself aroused the mayor's ire only once. Wagner, as mayor-elect, agreed to appoint the lame-duck Mayor Impellitteri a judge on a lower-court bench so that he could later qualify for a city pension. Wagner made the promise reluctantly, only consenting when the other members of the outgoing Board of Estimate, including Halley, urged it on him and pledged their public support if that proved necessary. Impellitteri, possibly to assure himself of continued consideration by the party, conferred shortly before he left office with Charles Buckley, Flynn's successor as Bronx boss (Impellitteri would not sit in the same room with De Sapio). As a result of the meeting, the outgoing mayor made two appointments to sinecures, one for a Buckley nominee and one for a De Sapio selection. Each appointment was for a term longer than that of the incoming mayor, and they were announced on Impellitteri's last day in City Hall. It looked like a deal, conditioned on Wagner's appointing Impellitteri to the judgeship.

Wagner, arriving at City Hall the next morning to be confronted with the *fait accompli,* stormed, "The bastards are selling me out before I've even got the seat warm." But he got over his fit of temper, swore in Impellitteri as a judge, and forgave De Sapio and Buckley for having taken the patronage jobs when Impellitteri offered them.

Apart from Gulick's, the most important appointment on which Wagner and De Sapio collaborated was that of police commissioner. The Police Department had been replete with publicized scandals in the O'Dwyer administration and with unpublicized ones under Impellitteri. Wagner and De Sapio were in immediate, total agree-

118

ment that as a matter of broad policy there would be no City Hall interference with the police in the Wagner administration; the Police Department would be run by its commissioner, and he would stand or fall on his own results. Their decision was political and pragmatic: the liabilities stemming from City Hall direction of police administration far outweighed any potential advantages.

When it came to discussing possible appointees as police commissioner, De Sapio came up with the man Wagner immediately realized was perfect for the job, Francis W. H. Adams. Adams had been U.S. attorney for the Southern District of New York, appointed by the nonpolitical federal judges to fill a vacancy. He had served with distinction there and later lent his name to Wagner's borough-presidential campaign as chairman of the Lawyers Committee for Wagner. Thus he had prestige, personality, and friendly relations with the new mayor.

Wagner named Adams, and his pledge of noninterference with the Police Department was sustained throughout his three city administrations, in relations with four successive commissioners. It represented a contrast with the preceding administration, in which appointments to the detective division of the Police Department were sold for cash and the payments made in City Hall.

Wagner's commissioners in his first two terms generally averaged out higher in capability than those of previous and even succeeding administrations (including his own third term and John Lindsay's) and many of them were found and dragooned into public service by the mayor's own outreach into the establishment, particularly in the health, welfare, and social service fields. Others were recommended by De Sapio, who knew what kind of man the mayor would want for each job. No matter who they were or whence they had come, De Sapio kept a benevolent eye on their operations in office, managing to be helpful in their staff problems without seeming to intrude as the boss.

The case of a top member of the mayor's City Hall staff exemplified the De Sapio technique. The man had been promoted after a year or so to a post he had sought outside the intimate City Hall orbit. Within a few months De Sapio felt that the aide was missed.

119

He tactfully enlisted the aid of Adrian Burke, by then a judge on the Court of Appeals, and the two together advised that the aide should be brought back. Wagner hated to think anyone was indispensable, but he compromised by recalling the man to City Hall on a part-time basis while retaining his new post, to function again as a member of the administrative cabinet in which he had been particularly effective.

Besides his hovering around the field of governmental operations, De Sapio had plenty to do in Wagner's first year as mayor simply as the mayor's one and only political agent. Acting for Wagner, he set things up for Brooklyn's Democrats to choose Joe Sharkey as their county chairman in succession to Kenneth Sutherland, who resigned even before the polls closed on the day Wagner was elected mayor. In Queens he achieved the ouster of the unfriendly Jim Roe and Roe's succession by Jim Phillips. No Manhattan boss before De Sapio had picked the leaders in other counties since the early years when Charlie Murphy picked the successive leaders of the Bronx, the last of whom was Flynn.

Buckley dropped into the role of junior partner that De Sapio had filled with Flynn. De Sapio himself inherited Flynn's membership on the Democratic national committee. This was a selection that could be made, in the event of a vacancy between national conventions, by the party's state committee, and De Sapio, with his handpicked city allies, controlled that body.

Acting as Wagner's agent, De Sapio took on the continuing chore of rounding up party support for Wagner programs in the City Council, the state legislature, and even Congress. Wagner felt it beneath the dignity of his office to pressure individual legislators, but also believed strongly that a man in legislative office should go along with the party platform and follow the party leadership. Legislators sometimes had to be reminded of their obligations, and it was De Sapio who herded reluctant lawmakers into line time and time again.

The boss also had to tie up loose ends in Tammany. A new state law abolished the right of a party to have unlimited membership on its county committee and imposed instead a restriction of from two to five members per election district. De Sapio saw to it that Tammany complied a full four months before the legal effective date. Tammany's county committee was reduced from 11,762 to 3,471, a much more workable number, but it also cut down the organization's year-round election manpower. He followed this by a change in the rules to provide for the direct election of district leaders by the enrolled party members, rather than by the county committee members. He hamstrung opposition to this among the district leaders by appealing to their own self-respect, telling them, "Any man who can't carry his own assembly district with his name on the ballot should not be the leader."

The words would return to haunt him.

In New York state the election for governor comes the year after the people of New York City pick their mayor. So De Sapio, while still engaged in city politics, had also to develop a winning candidate for the statewide race. With Tom Dewey giving up the governor's chair at last, the prospects of the Democrats having a winner looked good. Dewey, twice his party's losing presidential nominee, had always been formidable within the state. As John Crews, the Republican boss of Brooklyn, wisecracked at a dinner at which Dewey was guest of honor: "It's a funny thing about this guy Dewey. Every time he runs for President he gets reelected governor."

Even with Dewey out of the contest, De Sapio was taking no chances. To many, the Democratic Party's obvious choice was Franklin D. Roosevelt, Jr., an avowed candidate for the place his father had once held. As early as 1952 young Roosevelt had sat down with Bob Wagner, Jr., and the two agreed that their interests did not conflict, since Roosevelt wanted to be governor and Wagner to be mayor. They pledged each other support.

But Roosevelt was ill-advised enough to carry a message from Alex Rose of the Liberal Party to Wagner early in 1953, suggesting that Wagner drop out of contention for the mayoralty and take second place, the presidency of the City Council, on a ticket to be headed by Rudolph Halley and entered in both the Democratic and Liberal primaries. Wagner rejected the suggestion that he step aside for Halley and felt differently thereafter about Roosevelt. Roosevelt eventually supported Wagner in the Democratic primary, but Wagner felt he could remain neutral if there was an acceptable contender who opposed Roosevelt for the governorship.

As it turned out, De Sapio had reservations about Roosevelt. He considered him less than completely steady and reliable politically. There was much of his father in him, but less judgment and restraint as well. Also, young Roosevelt was in trouble with a substantial sector of the Roman Catholic community because of a controversy involving his mother. In the late 1940s there was pending in Congress the Barden bill, the first suggestion of substantial federal aid to education. In her role as a political activist, Eleanor Roosevelt supported the principle of the measure but demanded that no aid for parochial schools be permitted. Francis Cardinal Spellman, spokesman for the Roman Catholic Church in America, led the fight for inclusion of the church schools. The bill got nowhere in Congress, but outside of Congress there was name calling, with the cardinal making statements which attacked Mrs. Roosevelt personally.

All the public ever knew was that the cardinal "made up" with Mrs. Roosevelt by paying a call on her, for tea, at the family home in Hyde Park, a visit which was duly publicized. What never was printed was the fact that Ed Flynn had flown to Rome and laid the facts of the public quarrel before Pope Pius XII, whom Flynn had known when the then Cardinal Pacelli was papal secretary of state. Equally secretly, Cardinal Spellman was ordered to make a public gesture of friendship to Mrs. Roosevelt, and Cardinal Stritch of Chicago was designated to speak thereafter for the church in the area of public affairs.

However much the hierarchy of the church had settled the affair in Mrs. Roosevelt's favor, the rank and file of the Catholic community still resented the Roosevelt family, and Franklin Junior suffered the results. De Sapio began casting around for a gubernatorial candidate who would be less controversial. He checked with Wagner to see if the mayor was interested, but Wagner, in City Hall only six months, felt he could not leave without breaking faith with the people who had just elected him.

A logical candidate appeared in the person of Averell Harriman. He had tremendous experience and stature in national and international affairs. He also had a yen for the presidency which survived his failure to win the 1952 nomination. The governorship of New York is a traditional stepping stone toward presidential nomination, and Harriman let the fact that he was willing to make the gubernatorial race be known to both De Sapio and to Alex Rose of the Liberal Party, since the Liberal Party had always allied itself with the Democrats in statewide races.

Both De Sapio and Rose privately accepted the Harriman candidacy as preferable to that of young Roosevelt. They talked secretly with Mayor Wagner and Senator Lehman and persuaded them to accept Harriman.

De Sapio knew there would be an outcry of "boss rule" if he sprang the Harriman selection as a surprise. He therefore arranged for a joint statement by himself as national committeeman and Richard H. Balch of Utica as state chairman, concurred in by Wagner and Lehman, and issued two weeks before the state convention was to meet. It said:

Throughout the year and especially in the past two months the process of testing the qualifications and appeal of the various candidates by political analyses and consultations among party leaders has gone forward. This is the essence of the democratic process.

The purpose has been to ascertain and to recommend to the delegates to the convention the candidate best qualified to fill the office and best suited to present the Democratic record to the people of New York.

Senator Lehman and Mayor Wagner have taken part in the consultations and discussions, urging the party's organizational leaders to recommend a candidate clearly representative of the party's liberal traditions and clearly identified in the public mind with principle, integrity and achievement. Senator Lehman and Mayor Wagner had pledged themselves to support the party leadership if the candidate conformed to those requirements.

With less than two weeks before the convention, having taken counsel with party leaders in New York City and throughout the state, representing the overwhelming majority of the Democratic voters of the state, we [De Sapio and Balch] have agreed to recommend for the gubernatorial nomination the Honorable Averell Harriman, New York's favorite son for the Presidency in 1952 and an experienced statesman of national and world renown.

Based on the conclusions of the party leadership and without reflection on the high qualifications of other leading candidates, Senator Lehman and Mayor Wagner have expressed themselves as being wholly satisfied with this recommendation and have pledged their support to the nomination and election of this experienced, eminent and notable candidate.

The De Sapio maneuver had the effect of massing all of the party's heavy artillery behind the Harriman selection while absolving Lehman and Wagner from having initiated the move. Young Roosevelt took it hard, his mother even harder. On her own say-so to friends in the years that followed, she never forgave De Sapio "for what he did to my boy."

Herbert Lehman felt that the bruised feelings could be assuaged by giving Roosevelt a secondary place on the ticket, and he so advised De Sapio by telegram from a Pacific Coast vacation spot. De Sapio accordingly offered Roosevelt the nomination for state attorney general, even pressed it on him. Both De Sapio and Roosevelt appreciated that Harriman was already sixty-three years old and might well not seek a second term at sixty-seven if the presidency eluded him in the interim. Roosevelt could use these same four years in statewide office to increase his own prestige. Roosevelt accepted, reluctantly, the nomination for attorney general.

De Sapio checked out the entire ticket over the telephone with Wagner, who was not at the convention, but tied to his desk at City Hall. Wagner's only comment was that there was no Catholic on the ticket and that this could be corrected by nominating their friend and co-worker of the 1953 campaign, Adrian Burke, to the one unfilled spot, judge of the State Court of Appeals. De Sapio bought the idea wholeheartedly.

It was a good ticket, but the election that followed turned out to be far closer than anyone anticipated. Harriman should have had a comfortable 250,000 majority over Senator Irving M. Ives, the Republican selection. But the multimillionaire diplomat erred badly in handling the important issue of state aid to education. He endorsed a Wagner platform plank demanding more money for the city schools, without making it clear to the public that this would be done without taking money away from the upstate communities.

124

The Republicans leaped on the issue. They worked out a formula purporting to show how much each upstate community's aid would be cut and how much in additional taxes each town and village would have to raise to make up the difference, and they circulated the pertinent figures in every small community in the state. Harriman's entirely truthful protestations that he had proposed no such result were ignored by the rural voters. The Democratic upstate rural vote, never large anyhow, was reduced almost to zero in the hamlets and less populated townships, and Harriman squeaked through to election by a mere 11,000 majority.

For young Roosevelt the results were much more deflating. He lost by a wide margin and was the only loser on the ticket. Strangely enough, had he headed the ticket he might have won by more than Harriman. He would not have allowed his campaign to be derailed by a phony issue, and he undoubtedly would have received the solid vote of the New York City Jews, who did not vote for him for attorney general. They had used up their quota of philosophical liberalism in voting for Harriman for governor, and for the attorney generalship they turned to one of their own kind, a rising Republican named Jacob Javits. Roosevelt's defeat finished him as a factor in the Democratic Party.

Harriman's inability to straighten out the record on state aid for education was a warning signal of his inability to communicate with the people on bread-and-butter issues on the local level. Harriman, incredibly deft and informed in handling the nuances of world politics, had neither the background nor the patience for state politics. But this was ignored in the flush of the first Democratic state victory since 1938. And De Sapio received most of the praise for it.

Just as Wagner the year before had told a gathering at a Bronx County Democratic dinner that he owed his election to Buckley and De Sapio, so now did Averell Harriman hail De Sapio as "one of the great Democrats of our generation." He showed his appreciation, and his reliance on De Sapio's political generalship, by installing him as secretary of state, a purely ministerial office usually assigned to a party leader to permit him to devote most of his time to political problems and still earn a living. The office gave the occupant a cabinet-level salary, a car and chauffeur, and office space in New York, Albany, Buffalo, Rochester, Syracuse, Utica, and Binghamton, so that when on official business in any part of the state he could still do a bit of politicking while there.

Harriman's knowledge of state government and of the people who might be recruited for the top administrative and policy-making jobs did not measure up to Wagner's in the comparable city areas. So De Sapio played an even more important role in staffing the state-government machinery than he had at City Hall. He also dealt personally with the legislative leaders of the party in Albany and untangled problems which arose between Wagner and Harriman programs.

De Sapio did not give up his city connections and interests; in fact, at times he seemed to act as a Wagner ambassador at the Harriman court while performing his official and unofficial duties as counselor to the governor. No one questioned his dual role, and De Sapio never gave reason for it to be questioned. He had first elected a mayor and then a governor, was on intimate terms with each, and was trusted by each as the ultimate in political agentry. No political boss of either party had ever enjoyed such powers, and the prestige that inevitably accompanied them.

EIGHT

THE GOLDEN YEARS

The Harriman years as governor—1955 through 1958—were over-lapped by Wagner's continuing occupancy of City Hall. De Sapio, as the man who was responsible for the election of both governor and mayor, thus occupied for four years a position of power unequaled by any boss of either party in the current century. Charles F. Murphy had approached it during the period John F. Hylan was mayor and Al Smith was governor, but Hylan was just as much William Randolph Hearst's mayor as he was Murphy's.

De Sapio's status was what he must have dreamed about when he first adopted politics as his career and political leadership as his goal. He not only was looked to for his political decisions, but he acquired a broad and ever increasing audience for his political philosophy. He also developed the social graces befitting his new standing and prestige. His tailored silk suits were now quietly rather than loudly impressive. At important dinner parties he became relaxed and felt at ease, no longer the nervous young man in a cold sweat, literally watching his hostess for guidance on the use of silverware.

In public he was not only the boss, but the secretary of state of New York, who was entitled to a state-owned limousine and a state-paid chauffeur. He hardly ever availed himself of that particular luxury. He was sensitive to the public's irritability at indiscriminate use of government cars for private purposes, and the state limousine rolled up to the De Sapio door only on the days when the needs of his public office were to be met. There was another reason, too. The state limousine, with its low license plate, was easily identifiable, and the boss did not always want to advertise the political calls he was making. His schedule grew heavier and heavier, as he coped with political problems on both a city- and state-wide basis.

A normal day would start with brunch between 10:00 and 10:30 in the sunny breakfast room of the De Sapio apartment at 11 Fifth Avenue. There might be visitors at the table, discussing business that otherwise could not be squeezed in. Then the doorman would whistle up a taxicab, which would take De Sapio to the Biltmore headquarters. There would be conferences and appointments during the day, luncheons at which he sat and listened but never ate, and then a reasonably early dinner. If he had the time to permit the luxury, he ate at an Italian restaurant on West 48th Street, the Vesuvio, with his closest Tammany cronies, City Councilman John Merli and Assemblyman Frank Rossetti. Years later Rossetti would be the leader of what had been Tammany Hall.

Two nights a week there was a dinner table reserved for himself and the members of the Tammany executive committee in the Long-champs restaurant at 42nd Street and Lexington Avenue. It was De Sapio's way of indicating that he was not overlooking his original power base simply because he had gone on to broader areas of operations.

Whether he was dining for pleasure at Vesuvio or for business at Longchamps, he was a hearty eater, stoking up for the night's work, which would include attending three, or four, or five political dinners scattered in and about the five boroughs. Since he did not drive and would not use the state car after working hours, he would travel in a private car owned and chauffeured by Rossetti, Merli, or another crony. At each stop he would shake hands, take a seat on the dais, speak briefly when called upon, and hurry off to the next appointment. He never was finished before midnight.

De Sapio enjoyed meeting the people, he enjoyed the acclaim that was his. Later there were friends who felt that some of the mistakes he made were founded on an overdose of confidence which stemmed from the public plaudits. It certainly was true that as he lectured incessantly on the respectability and desirability of responsible political leadership, he was heard with attention by the general public and in the academic world.

Adlai Stevenson, Democratic nominee for President in 1952 and still the idol of the party liberals in 1955, had no hesitation in declaring, "If I were to seek the Democratic nomination in 1956, I would welcome the support of Carmine De Sapio and Tammany Hall." Stevenson, of course, was seeking the 1956 nomination and wanted the important New York State delegation in his corner, just as others had wanted it in the past, but no previous aspirant had ever so publicly embraced a Tammany Hall leader. It seemed, for a time, as though Tammany Hall was no longer the whipping boy in national presidential politics.

What Stevenson said publicly, others of his philosophy were saying in private. Stanley Lowell, in describing years later De Sapio's position vis-à-vis the party's liberal or intellectual wing, said, "He was the only leader we would go to for help on liberal, substantive issues. Carmine was not an intellectual, but he was in every sense a pragmatic liberal."

On the issue of racial minorities, which was to become so important within the Democratic Party, De Sapio was well ahead of his contemporaries elsewhere. In Manhattan the gerrymandering of the black territories came to an end. The number of black district leaders on the executive committee increased in number, and they were treated as equals. He saw to it that the first Puerto Rican district leader was seated on the committee as early as 1954, and he kept the need for minority representation in mind as he made patronage recommendations to both the mayor and the governor.

Fraternal and eleemosynary groups which had hesitated in the past to extend recognition to politicians heaped their awards on De Sapio. He received "man of the year" type citations from the Federation of Jewish Philanthropies, the Knights of Columbus, the American Legion, the Veterans of Foreign Wars, and half a dozen groups within the Italian community. Capturing a celebrity to be the guest of honor at a dinner or a luncheon is a time-honored method of fund raising. In De Sapio's case he was the "victim" as often as not, but even so, it reflected his acceptance by the community at large as a leading citizen who had made practical politics a successful and honorable career. He went few places in public without drawing a crowd of well-wishers, men and women who wanted to shake his hand in the kind of tribute usually paid only to popular holders of high elective office.

His association with Harriman brought him into contact with social and international figures. The diplomat-turned-governor had De Sapio to lunch or dinner at the Harriman townhouse, on one occasion to join in honoring a British Labour Party leader, where De Sapio shared a table with Grayson Kirk, president of Columbia University, and Ambassador Chester Bowles, just back from a tour of duty in India. De Sapio himself was the host at a dinner at the 21 Club—the old speakeasy converted into a fashionable bistro—for a group of men who would figure prominently in the 1960 round of President making, among them Senator Stuart Symington of Missouri; David Lawrence, the Pennsylvania boss; Mayor Thomas D'Alessandro of Baltimore; Governor Dennis Roberts of Rhode Island; and Democratic National Chairman Paul Butler of Indiana.

Jake Arvey, the boss of Illinois, and Jesse Unruh, then a rising power in California politics, were among others who made up the party of twenty-five. Host De Sapio chartered a bus to take the group from the dinner table to ringside at Yankee Stadium to see a heavyweight championship fight. It was one of De Sapio's rare displays of ostentation. He was indulging himself, for he enjoyed a good prizefight, and attended frequently.

When De Sapio first discussed with Harriman the idea of Harriman's running for governor, there was an implied commitment that he would back Harriman for the presidential nomination in 1956. De Sapio carried it out openly and vigorously—despite the bid from Stevenson—and made trips in Harriman's behalf as far as the Pacific Coast. He was well received personally wherever he went, but Harriman's candidacy evoked politeness rather than enthusiasm. De Sapio himself was making national contacts he hoped to use in 1960.

The road De Sapio traveled outside his home state had been paved for him by nationwide publicity depicting him as a new type of leader who stood for a new kind of clean machine politics. Feature stories in the big newspaper cities—Chicago, Cleveland, Kansas City, Atlanta, Los Angeles—told of the handsome, well-dressed Tammany boss who preached and practiced both politics and reform. Sunday

130

supplements delighted in the seeming contradiction of his spotless record as a political boss and the titillating air of mystery that his dark glasses bestowed. *Time, Life, Newsweek,* the *Saturday Evening Post, Fortune, Harper's,* and the *Atlantic* printed pieces which, sometimes laudatory, sometimes tongue-in-cheek, all contributed to the recognition of De Sapio as a force on the national scene. *Harper's* entitled its interpretative article "The Smile on the Face of the Tiger."

De Sapio lectured at Ivy League colleges, where his message was that participation in politics means being a good citizen. He argued that the voters owed it to themselves to support responsible party leadership that would direct the party along the road of progress that the voters themselves sought. On occasion he was specific: in an article in the Harvard Law *Record* he stressed the need for a constitutional convention in New York to update the state charter; for legislative reapportionment, so that the lawmakers would better reflect the will of the people; for a modernized court system; and for greater home rule for the cities. All, incidentally, were Democratic program planks adopted by the party under his leadership, but no one could recall a party boss so publicly demonstrating interest in legislation and reforms.

The thinking and the tone of De Sapio's articles and speeches were his own, but he had two "ghosts" to do the actual writing. One was George Hamilton Combs, a radio broadcaster long involved personally in Tammany politics. Combs put together the more scholarly articles. The second, far better known as a De Sapio aide, was a brilliant and brassy public relations man named Sydney Baron, who had no previous background in New York politics but who attached himself to De Sapio in 1953 and never let go.

In personality and tactics Baron made the Hollywood press agent of legend seem wan and retiring. No stunt was too wild for Baron to contemplate, no language too lurid for at least the first draft of a speech. When a story was leaked to the press in the 1953 mayoralty primary that De Sapio's life had been threatened and De Sapio appeared in public with a bodyguard, cynics suspected that this was Baron's way of getting across the point that some of the underworld were backing Impellitteri. A top-flight pro in public relations, Baron had all of the assets and liabilities appropriate to his trade, and to a greater degree than most.

There were those who thought Baron pushed De Sapio too far into the limelight, that sooner or later he would get into trouble as a result of too much publicity. Buckley, the earthy Bronx boss, repeatedly told De Sapio, "Why the hell don't you stick to your knitting, which is politics, and keep your mug out of the newspapers? Stay away from those lecture platforms, too. You don't need them."

Those who thought Baron's brashness would eventually reflect on the boss were able to say "I told you so" when it was disclosed in 1957 that Baron had taken on as a public relations client the bloody-handed dictator of the Dominican Republic, Rafael Trujillo, whose policies were anathema to Democratic Party liberals in New York. Franklin D. Roosevelt, Jr., had already learned that lesson, to his sorrow, when he briefly held the Trujillo account.

Besides being De Sapio's personal agent, Baron in 1957 was also official press representative for Tammany Hall, the first one it ever had. When the Baron link to Trujillo was disclosed, De Sapio knew Baron had to go as Tammany's press man. What followed was a typical De Sapio-arranged series of actions. The suggestion that Baron retire from his Tammany post was made, not by De Sapio, but by Governor Harriman. Mayor Wagner then publicly concurred, and then so did De Sapio. Baron, who possibly participated himself in the timing of the sequence, expressed effusively and publicly his regrets at having embarrassed his "dear friend Carmine," resigned the Tammany post, and continued writing De Sapio's speeches.

De Sapio's reputation was bruised less by the Baron incident than by the "money in the taxicab" episode which came within weeks of the first.

One July morning in 1957 De Sapio hailed a taxicab at Fifth Avenue and Eighth Street, a few steps from his apartment, and had the driver take him to the Biltmore. After De Sapio departed, the cab driver spotted a white envelope, held together with Scotch tape, on the passenger seat. The driver opened it and found nothing but money—money that eventually counted out to $11,200 in $50 and

$100 bills. The bills were dirty and faded and musty, as though they had long been buried in some dank place.

The driver turned in the envelope at the nearest police station, along with a description of his last passenger, a tall, well-dressed man in dark glasses. De Sapio readily identified himself as the man who had ridden in the cab from the Village to the Biltmore, but denied that the money was his or that he knew anything about it. It must have been on the seat of the cab when he entered, he maintained, and he was so preoccupied with thoughts of other matters that he had not noticed it.

No claimant of the money ever appeared, and a year later, in accordance with the police lost-and-found regulations, it became the property of the honest cab driver. In the interval the newspapers had a field day, printing the cab driver's description of "the man in the dark glasses"; repeating the driver's statement that if an envelope had been on the back seat before he picked up De Sapio he would have noticed it; and reviving the whole affair periodically to report that no person had appeared to claim the money. Only when the year's grace period had expired and the cabbie got the money, and not before, was the incident ended.

Most people in politics assumed it was De Sapio's money. Those who knew him well understood from experience that he was perfectly capable of leaving a package of papers—or money—anyplace. He carried his memorandums of "contracts" on tiny bits of paper scattered through his pockets and was constantly fishing through them to find the memorandum wanted at the moment. There were many occasions when he could not find the appropriate memo, and if he could remember who gave it to him, had to call back and ask for the details all over again.

The people who assumed it was De Sapio's money assumed also that he did not claim it because he did not want to have to explain its source or his possession of it. What puzzled many was the conflict between the unexplained cash and De Sapio's record as they knew it. Throughout his association with the Wagner and Harriman administrations De Sapio had not been involved in any scandal, nor were there any private rumblings that hooked him up with anything illegitimate. Wagner, years later, was to tell intimates that he never detected, or even heard a rumor of, a single situation in which it appeared that De Sapio was involved in any corruption. A mayor has long ears and many listening devices, and Wagner's comment was made years after he had publicly split with his former partner.

Sophisticates in politics are aware that cash changes hands more than checks in the political world, sometimes even when the purpose is legitimate, like a campaign contribution, but which has a tinge of illegitimacy because there is knowledge on both sides that the contribution will not figure in the formal reports of campaign expenditures.

In the case of the money in the taxicab, because of the odd amount involved it could easily have represented the price of promotion of a lower-court judge to a higher court. But no one could venture an explanation of the musty odor and dank condition of the currency itself.

Harry Hershfield, the professional jester and master of ceremonies, who was a close friend of De Sapio, set his hearers to laughing with his remark, "That couldn't possibly be Carmine's money —not that neat, clean Carmine and those dirty old bills."

Certainly there was no change as a result of the incident in the relationship of De Sapio to the governor and the mayor. Nor did it figure importantly in the 1957 mayoralty election campaign only a few months later, in which Wagner set an all-time record for popular approval of an administration. As the nominee of the Democratic, Liberal, and City Fusion parties, Wagner polled 1,508,775 votes, against 585,768 for Robert K. Christenberry, the Republican sacrificial lamb who was his sole opponent. The vote of endorsement for the Wagner record was not only by far the largest ever received by any candidate for mayor; it was a plurality 50 percent greater than a winner had ever received even against divided opposition.

De Sapio played a large part in the running of the reelection campaign, but it is doubtful that he approved a campaign pledge Wagner made, which was to cut down the mayor's freedom of political choice thereafter. Wagner had gone to the 1956 Democratic national convention—which renominated Stevenson over feeble opposition from the Harriman camp—committed to Stevenson and openly seeking the vice-presidential nomination for himself. This willingness of Wagner to abandon the mayoralty for the vice-presidency left him ideologically unable to resist a genuine draft for the U.S. Senate seat that Herbert Lehman was relinquishing because of his advancing years.

Wagner had always nourished an ambition to succeed to his father's old chair in the Senate, but with Eisenhower running for reelection and Stevenson a re-tread nominee, weaker than he had been four years earlier, to make a 1956 race for the Senate in New York was hopeless. Nevertheless, Wagner found it impossible to dismiss the entreaties of Lehman and Eleanor Roosevelt that he make the race to strengthen the Stevenson chances.

Wagner lost by 400,000 but made a creditable run, polling a million more votes than Stevenson statewide. The echoes of that lost battle carried over into the next campaign, and the press hounded Wagner for an unequivocal answer to the question whether or not after his reelection as mayor he would run for the second Senate seat in 1958. Never the type to shout back at anyone, including the members of the press, Wagner allowed himself to be bullied into a pledge that he would serve out his full term as mayor and thus would seek no other office before 1961.

This ill-considered pledge by Wagner—which he did not need to get himself reelected in 1957—handicapped Wagner in thinking of his own future, and De Sapio in planning for one. Neither as yet was too worried about a storm cloud on the horizon. This was the reform movement within the Democratic Party. It had been born after World War II of a yearning for political participation by a new generation of voters and was tied in closely during the 1950s with the adulation of Adlai Stevenson by the party's liberal wing in New York. There had been a reform movement centering in the New York Young Democratic Club, which William O'Dwyer had used in 1949 as a drum to beat out his public discord with Tammany, but it was too diffused throughout Manhattan as a whole to have real strength or lasting power. The durable reform movement got its start that same year in a single district, the fashionable 9th A.D., which took in the Park Avenue section.

Wealthy young men and women, who had time as well as money to devote to the project, formed, financed, and popularized their own district club, the Lexington Democratic Club, and it quickly became formidable opposition for the Grover Cleveland Democratic Club, the regular Tammany organization in the area. The movement spread to other districts, for the same reason it succeeded along Park Avenue: when newcomers went to their local clubs to join and participate actively, they found no welcome mats on the doorsteps. James E. Lanigan, later the David who slew the Goliath De Sapio in his home district, frequently related what happened to him when he went to a Tammany club, dues in hand, to apply for membership. "Save your five dollars, kid," he was told. "We'll get in touch with you if we need you."

The regular clubs, no longer accustomed to an annual influx of recruits, wanted none at all, particularly young activists who could prove troublemakers. So liberal Democrats all over the county, seeking a place in the party structure, either had to give up the idea or give up on the existing clubs, and start their own. They chose the second course and formed their own loosely coordinated machine. The Lexington Club furnished manpower and election-law and procedural guidance to most of the other clubs at the beginning, until ideological differences developed.

The Lexington Club was generally committed to the limited goal of supporting selected individuals for party and public office rather than simply opposing all machine nominees. Later comers to the reform movement felt that the proper procedure was to wage unremitting warfare on the machine, backing anyone who opposed it, any place, for any office. Their viewpoint eventually prevailed.

The Lexington Club crowd scored their first victory in 1952, electing Lloyd K. Garrison, a Stevenson law partner, and Mrs. Dorothy Schiff, the millionaire owner and publisher of the *New York Post,* to membership on the Democratic state committee, and the following year the group consolidated its hold on the area by electing Jean J. P. Baltzell and Alice Sachs to the Tammany Hall executive committee as district leader and co-leader respectively.

De Sapio had, of course, backed his own Tammany 9th A.D.

organization, but as soon as the Garrison-Schiff ticket scored its victory in 1952 he greeted the reformers with the statement: "I look forward to their serving on the Democratic state committee as true Democrats who will encourage the progressive policies of the party and will keep on fostering a real people's program."

For the first decade of the reform movement De Sapio never hesitated to accept as party regulars any of the reformers who were willing to accept him. In 1951, even before the Lexington Club victory, he had combined forces in selected areas with the reformers to accomplish the defeat of regular members of the executive committee who were pro-Impellitteri. Two such deals paved the way for the team of Herbert De Varco and Estelle Karpf as leader and co-leader from midtown, and Will Midonick and Margot Gayle from Chelsea.

De Sapio, as ever, was playing practical politics and certainly did not overlook the presence in the reform movement of so many political "fat cats" who could not only finance a winning ticket in a district but would support city, state, and national candidates generously if welcomed inside the party.

However, welcoming words from him as leader of Tammany Hall were unconvincing to the reformer rank and file, particularly the Stevenson rooters who could not bring themselves to believe that their idol would have fared as badly as he did in 1952 if he had been given true support from the organization. The Stevensonians were very much like the young men and women who went to the polls for the first time in 1940 to vote for Wendell Willkie as the Republican nominee. They identified with their choice, in their first taste of politics, and they wanted Stevenson again. De Sapio's backing of Harriman in the 1956 campaign, while reform organizing was still going on, made them more determined in their independence of the existing Tammany organization, regardless of the protestations of its leader.

Richard Brown, later the directing genius of the reform movement as a united anti-De Sapio movement, recalls that during the 1952 presidential campaign he went to De Sapio in his own capacity as New York director of the Stevenson Volunteers and urged that the volunteers be permitted to carry on joint canvassing and propagandizing of the voters with the regular Tammany clubs, to avoid needless duplication of effort. De Sapio gave the idea his blessing and passed it on to the district leaders, but when it came to the test only De Sapio's own Tamawa Club let down the barriers to the amateurs. The other clubs would not even make literature available to the volunteers. And De Sapio, in 1952, did not yet have the power to make his word Tammany's law.

The second defeat of Stevenson in the 1956 election served to encourage rather than deter the political zeal of his Manhattan followers. The Village Independent Democrats, known familiarly as the VID, started out in 1957 in De Sapio's own district, in opposition to his Tamawa Club. While some of the reform clubs were activist and others were debating societies, the VID stood out as distinct from any other group. They were a particularly stubborn collection of individualists who seemed never to be able to agree on anything, much less how to organize effectively for political action. Jim Lanigan, after he had run on the VID ticket, characterized them as "a hard core of inflexible dialecticians who somehow believe they have a monopoly on truth."

The VID group was the first to be avowedly anti-De Sapio—as opposed to reform as a general goal—and it was one of the few things on which their noisy membership meetings could find agreement, but it was not taken too seriously by their fellow reform organizations, or by De Sapio, their primary target. Thus it was surprising that in the first test of VID strength in De Sapio's home area, the VID candidate for leader, Herman Greitzer, got as much as 37 percent of the vote, against 63 percent for De Sapio, in an extraordinary primary turnout of 40 percent of the eligible Democrats.

De Sapio brushed off the result as a freak. He counted on his own well-established image as a man sympathetic to reform to keep the official reform movement under control. After all, he reasoned, without his reforms in the election process, including the direct election of district leaders, the opposition would have found it difficult even to get on the ballot.

NINE

TROUBLE

P olitical history is full of examples of how events at nominating conventions determine the results of the election months later. It is almost axiomatic that the circumstances surrounding the nomination of a candidate determine his reception by the public.

In 1912 President William Howard Taft won renomination at a Republican national convention by using his control of the party machinery to unseat enough of Teddy Roosevelt's delegates to give the Taft forces a majority. As a result, Taft finished third in November. In 1924 the Democrats entered their Madison Square Garden convention hopeful of winning the presidency on the wave of revelations of Teapot Dome and other scandals of the Harding administration. But the Democrats split wide open on the issue of denunciation of the resurgent Ku Klux Klan and on the Protestant candidacy of William Gibbs McAdoo versus the Catholic candidacy of Alfred E. Smith. The eventual nominee, John W. Davis, never had a chance in the election that followed. In 1968 the tone of the proceedings inside the Chicago convention hall, and the rioting and bludgeoning that went on outside, handicapped Hubert Humphrey from start to finish.

In New York state politics there were landmark Democratic conventions in 1922, 1932, 1942, and 1958. Events at the first two presaged success, at the latter two they paved the path to defeat. For Carmine De Sapio the state convention held in Buffalo in September 1958 was what the Russian campaign of 1812 was to Napoleon. His leadership of the Democratic Party survived an additional three years, but was under constant challenge. For the Democratic Party as a whole, the Buffalo developments spelled defeat and dissension for at least a dozen years thereafter.

There is a basic difference between the Buffalo convention and the other landmark conventions, either state or national. In all but Buffalo the public was informed of what went on. The 1912 Taft-Roosevelt fight took place in the open, with every detail reported by an avid press. The 1924 Madison Square Garden battle was the first ever broadcast on the radio, and the whole nation heard the horrible details for the three full weeks that it lasted. The 1968 Chicago convention of the Democrats dominated every television screen.

At the state level the 1922 drama took place in Al Smith's private hotel room, but the press found ways to inform the public of how Smith, the party's chief hope of recapturing the governorship, refused to run on the same ticket with that "s.o.b." William Randolph Hearst, whom Boss Murphy was trying to give Smith as his running mate, and of how Murphy capitulated and Hearst quit. In 1932 reporters similarly reported accurately what went on behind closed doors: the insistence of Smith and Franklin Roosevelt that the bosses nominate Herbert Lehman for governor, and how the bosses gave in. In 1942 a battle between Jim Farley and the man he had guided into the presidency, Franklin Roosevelt, for control of the New York state wing of the party was carried out on the convention floor, and more than adequately reported by a tremendous press and radio corps.

At Buffalo the fight that broke up the Democratic Party was waged behind closed doors. The results of the disagreement among the leaders reached the public, but not the causes or the details. The press corps was weak, most of the first-string reporters having been assigned to the Republican convention, where the first appearance of Nelson A. Rockefeller as a political candidate seemed to warrant the spotlight. The one top-ranking political reporter rushed to Buffalo after the close of the Democratic convention happened to be one who was notoriously more at home with Republicans than with Democrats. His news sources at Buffalo were limited. But he had been rushed over by his paper, *The New York Times,* to give its readers the inside story, and what he could not find out—which was most of it—he concocted. He pictured De Sapio as defying both Harriman and Wagner, and reported that Wagner had threatened De Sapio with the loss of patronage and that De Sapio in return threatened to take control of the city Board of Estimate away from the mayor. De Sapio did defy Harriman, but Wagner's role was that of interested spectator, and the reported threats of reprisal were sheer fantasy. There was no split at Buffalo between the mayor and the boss.

However, the *Times* had a reputation for accuracy in political reporting, and its detailed report of the boss-ridden conclave was accepted as factual. It contributed heavily to the party defeat in the election two months later. That version of Buffalo has never been challenged up to now.

Actually the architects of the disaster were three men, only one of whom was a political boss. They were Governor Harriman, who displayed incredible political ineptness and naiveté in the six months preceding the convention; Mayor Wagner, who let completely justified personal pique and irritation with Harriman stand in the way of party peace and his own elevation to the Senate; and Carmine De Sapio, who came to the convention prepared to run the show while insisting on disclaiming the boss role, a display of double-talk which deceived no one.

De Sapio's role was the only one that was evident on the surface, and as a result he was handed the blame for the defeat of the party's nominees for governor and senator. De Sapio, trying to overrule the governor without losing his standing with him, played a two-faced role, but otherwise the charges against him were too sweeping and the situation oversimplified. For example, the loss of the governorship. Harriman was finishing a term in office in which he had failed to identify with a major issue. While every other governor of modern times, except the Republican Nathan L. Miller in 1922, had been reelected to office as often as he sought it, Harriman would probably have been defeated by the rising young Nelson Rockefeller even if there had been no contention at Buffalo.

On the other hand, the Democrats would have won the Senate

seat. Wagner, to whom it was offered, could have easily been elected over the then unknown Kenneth B. Keating, and Frank Hogan, the actual nominee, lost only by a little, despite open sabotage of his candidacy by most of the Democratic reform movement. The reformers seized eagerly on the boss issue presented to them by the press and kept it alive throughout the campaign. They preferred a downgrading of De Sapio to a seat for his choice in the Senate.

Actually De Sapio and his allies, who controlled a majority of the convention delegates at Buffalo, played no more dominating a role than they or their predecessors had played at any state convention of either major party in the half-century from 1918 to 1968, when the convention system was the exclusive method of making party nominations for statewide office. All of the nominees of this era, good, bad, and indifferent, were boss-picked.

The old state convention resembled a national convention both in form and practice. It was an assembly of approximately 1,000 delegates, with the quota from each county determined by the vote cast in that county for the party nominee for governor in the previous election. In the Democratic Party this format meant that the convention was controlled by the counties containing large cities. The delegates were picked, theoretically, in a primary, but actually by the party machine in the area, and they were expected to follow the leadership of the local boss in a showdown vote.

The convention system, rather than the direct primary, was mandated by the state election law—written by the major party representatives in the legislature—because it enabled the party bosses to sit around a table in a hotel suite on the night before the convention and privately reconcile their differences. They usually emerged from the room with a "balanced" state ticket which they "recommended" and which the delegates thereafter approved without dissent.

The editorial-page concept that such a ticket was automatically boss-ridden simply because of its parentage had little real validity. The concern of the men locked in the privacy of the conference room was the selection of a set of winning candidates, without which their own status as party bosses would be diminished. It follows that the demands of the voters who would have to be wooed between the convention and the election constituted the principal guide for the conferees. They would pick the men they thought the people wanted—or could be convinced that they wanted—with a minimal concern for their personal predilections. The procedure looked completely undemocratic, but in practice its choices were more of a party consensus than those produced since by the direct statewide primary.

Looking back over the fifty years of convention-picked nominees of both major parties, it is impossible to find one who was named because he would make a more controllable officeholder than some stronger candidate who did not please the bosses. They never cast aside a sure winner. The convention system produced a long list of outstanding public servants who were popular as well—Al Smith, Franklin Roosevelt, Herbert Lehman, and Robert F. Wagner, Sr., among the Democrats; Tom Dewey, Nelson Rockefeller, Irving Ives, and Jacob K. Javits in the Republican ranks. It also produced some mediocrities, in fact was almost certain to do so in any year when the party appeared headed for defeat no matter whom it selected.

The bosses liked the convention system because it enabled them to heal party rifts. In the privacy of the room each county boss heard the arguments of the others, had his own say, and eventually concurred in the verdict. Any elder statesman of the party was always welcome to attend.

A classic example of wound binding in private took place at the Democratic convention of 1932, when whoever was nominated was sure to be elected. The boss of Tammany Hall, John F. Curry, headed a coalition of county bosses which controlled a majority of the convention votes, exactly as De Sapio did at Buffalo in 1958. Curry, who had his own candidate for the job, was opposing the promotion of Lehman, then lieutenant governor, to succeed Governor Franklin Roosevelt, who was on his way to the presidency.

Al Smith, the revered elder statesman, was fighting hard for Lehman, who had always contributed generously to Smith's campaigns. He leaned across the table and said to Curry, "If you don't go along with Lehman, I'll take the party away from you by running for mayor of New York next year."

"On what ticket?" sneered Curry.

"On a Chinese laundry ticket I could beat you and your crowd," Smith retorted.

Curry knew Smith spoke the truth, that he could never best the great former governor in a contest for the support of New York City voters. He threw in his cards, and there was no fight on the floor of the state convention. Lehman was nominated and was supported by Tammany on election day that year and on each of the six successive occasions that he ran for governor or U.S. senator.

At Buffalo there was a formal roll call, on which every delegate had to be counted as for Harriman, or for De Sapio, or for reform. It was De Sapio who eventually pressed the button for the countdown, but it was Harriman who paved the way for it.

Harriman started cultivating trouble within the party as early as the preceding March. Habitually impatient in dealing with petty things like state politics, Harriman had sent for De Sapio unusually early to discuss what lay ahead in the November election. The governor made it clear to the party boss—his own appointee as secretary of state—that he was a candidate for another four years as governor and thought that the ticket should be balanced by the nomination of a Catholic for U.S. senator. The seat was the one being given up by the Republican Irving M. Ives, whom Harriman had defeated for governor in 1954. Harriman's thinking hardly came as a surprise to De Sapio until, shaking a forefinger under De Sapio's nose, he added, "But I don't want that Wagner on the ticket."

De Sapio was on the spot. Harriman was the man he had made governor, Wagner was the man he had made mayor. He wanted no quarrel between them, though he had no idea if Wagner wanted to run. So he stalled. He suggested it was still very early in the political year, that there was plenty of time for consideration of Harriman's running mates. His maneuver worked only for a short while.

A few weeks later Harriman again summoned his political chieftain and wanted to know what progress had been made in developing a ticket. He again waved the forefinger as he stated he didn't want the nominee for senator to be Wagner. He backed up his position by saying that Wagner would hurt the ticket, because of the scandals in the Wagner city administration.

144

De Sapio suggested that the scandals being played up in the press involved nothing more serious than the taking of five- and ten-dollar bills by inspectors in the Buildings Department—a perennial headache to any administration—and that the press would eventually give up trying to make political capital of the issue. He told Harriman he did not know if Wagner was even interested in running for the Senate, and suggested that Harriman talk over the situation with the mayor himself. Harriman, only temporarily convinced on the scandal issue, agreed to talk to the mayor.

De Sapio, back in New York City, hinted at some difficulties with Harriman that the mayor might clear up, but he did not spell them out. So Wagner dropped in on the governor at his beach house at Sands Point, on the way to his own summer home at Islip. The two men were alone. The governor made it clear to the mayor that he regarded Wagner's nomination for the Senate as inadvisable. The mayor made it equally clear that he had not been a candidate for the Senate in the first place.

The episode left Wagner miffed at Harriman, and the party without a possibility for the Senate who was readily acceptable to the party leadership. It also set De Sapio to reviewing his whole relationship with Harriman. In 1952, as a junior member of the party hierarchy, he had gone to the Democratic national convention supporting Harriman as New York's favorite-son candidate for the presidency. At the 1956 convention, as the party's ruling boss, he had again supported Harriman for President. Harriman lost out each time, but that had not mattered too much, since no Democrat could have defeated Dwight Eisenhower in the election. On the other hand, 1960 loomed as a probable winning year for the party and De Sapio wanted to be a factor in the naming of the presidential nominee, to control the delegation to the national convention.

In this ambition he could count on no help from Harriman or his personal staff. If reelected governor, Harriman would regard himself as still a presidential possibility, even though the realities called for a younger man. His staff could be counted upon to sharpen the governor's appetite for the national office.

Harriman did not have a great staff. De Sapio felt—and many

others agreed—that most of the men closest to Harriman were long on advice but short on the wisdom and capacity to implement it. Some of them irritated him additionally because they had cast their lot with the reform movement in Manhattan—opposed to De Sapio's role as party boss—but worked with him on the state level, where their jobs were directly involved. He mentally tabbed them as "nit pickers" and blamed them for such boners as Harriman's premature and unnecessary ruling out of Wagner as a running mate. He felt that the governor was so divorced from the realities of state politics that he was unable to differentiate between good counsel and bad.

De Sapio resolved, sometime in 1958, to assert his own leadership, looking ahead to 1960, but making the picking of the 1958 ticket a symbol. It is certain that when he set about creating the coalition of county bosses which would control the Senate nomination of 1958, he intended to maintain it as a unit which would decide whom New York backed for President at the next national convention.

Harriman, on his own, decided to back Thomas E. Murray, Jr., as his senatorial running mate. Murray, a wealthy engineer and inventor, was a member of the Atomic Energy Commission and was also a papal knight, an honor bestowed in recognition of his substantial financial contributions to the Catholic Church. The combination appealed to Harriman, and he thought it would also appeal to the voters. He turned his attention to the preliminary step of "selling" Murray to the party leadership, without making a formal public announcement of his decision.

The governor persuaded Mayor Wagner to arrange for the five county chairmen from New York City to meet with Murray so that they could size him up. To give status to the meeting, it was held in De Sapio's state office suite at 270 Broadway, across the street from City Hall. The city leaders who attended, including De Sapio, were unimpressed. They did not assess Murray as a choice that would stimulate popular support and add strength to the ticket. Murray's governmental career consisted of his AEC commissionership and nothing more; he was not known personally in the state outside of high church circles; and physically he did not look as though he were

146

up to the kind of campaigning that would be necessary to make himself better known. The diagnosis was correct, events proved, for Murray was already suffering from an incurable ailment that killed him two and a half years later at a relatively early age.

Murray failed to impress at similar meetings arranged by Harriman upstate, and De Sapio made his own decision to back District Attorney Hogan for the Senate. He quickly assembled the other city leaders and a majority of the bosses of the upstate counties in support of his position. They foresaw no great popular surge for Murray, and were willing to follow the leadership of De Sapio, thus far successful in the choices he had made. Whether De Sapio discussed with any of them the look ahead he had taken at 1960 is not known.

De Sapio wanted no public rupture with Harriman, nor the governor with him, and so for a substantial period preceding the Buffalo convention De Sapio worked to preserve the fiction that he had no candidate of his own for the Senate, and at the convention itself he could picture the Hogan candidacy as coming spontaneously from the other county leaders who were his allies, in fact his subordinates.

The word of the Hogan candidacy spread privately, but not in the press. Hogan called on Mayor Wagner at Gracie Mansion; so did Tom Murray. Both separately told the mayor they were candidates for the Senate but would withdraw if Wagner wanted the seat himself. Wagner told both he would not let his name be considered.

Three days before the Buffalo convention De Sapio was visited by Alex Rose, the Liberal Party boss who expected to nominate whomever the Democrats picked, and he was accompanied by George Backer, Harriman's millionaire brain-truster. Rose and Backer urged the nomination of Thomas K. Finletter for the Senate. Backer's sponsorship of Finletter reflected the confusion within the governor's camp. The governor wanted Murray, his closest friend was pushing Finletter, and his political agent was backing Hogan.

Finletter, an activist in the New York City reform movement, had served as Secretary of the Air Force in the last two years of the Truman administration and had been politically ambitious thereafter. He and Harriman had crossed paths frequently in their Washington careers and disliked each other intensely. Moreover Finletter, by 1958 a law partner of Adlai Stevenson, was obviously going to support a third nomination for Stevenson in 1960, which did not fit in with Harriman's idea of becoming the candidate himself.

Harriman had allowed himself to be persuaded by Backer to make an announcement that he would be satisfied with the nomination of either Murray or Finletter, which regularized Backer's approach to De Sapio in Finletter's behalf, but in the overall picture Harriman's announcement that he would take either man served to dilute the strength either one could muster. In any event, De Sapio told Rose and Backer that the Senate race was wide open, that he had no candidate of his own, although, of course, he did not endorse Finletter.

On Sunday night, the eve of the convention, Rose was in Buffalo at Harriman's invitation. He conferred again with De Sapio, and asked, "What's this I hear about Hogan being all set for the nomination, that nobody else is being considered?"

De Sapio replied, "You haven't heard it from me, have you?"

To Rose, this was dissimulation, which had previously been foreign to his discussions with the Democratic Party chief. It reflected, of course, De Sapio's attempt to have the Hogan support appear to be coming from others, and accepted by him only in the spirit of majority rule. If Governor Harriman did not know better, Mayor Wagner did.

Buckley, the Bronx boss, arrived at the convention scene early, to start oiling the machinery for the Hogan nomination. He dropped in on Wagner in the mayor's hotel suite on Sunday afternoon, and told him that he would support him for senator, if the mayor was interested. Wagner said he was not, but to show he was aware of what was going on, he remarked that he knew Buckley was operating in De Sapio's behalf to secure votes for Hogan. Buckley admitted that to be a fact, but repeated that Wagner was still his own first choice.

It is likely that Buckley was making a last-minute check for De Sapio, to make sure that Wagner would not make the Senate race, for if he was willing, the signals would have to be changed.

Sunday night and Monday brought the delegates, and their wives and camp followers. They milled around the hotel lobbies, as tradition dictated, waiting for "the word"; accepting the latest rumor as fact, passing it on with embellishment. But the word was long in coming, and the rumors were even more unfounded than usual, because there were fewer men locked up in the conference room and thus there were fewer leaks. The principal conferees were just four in number: the governor; the mayor of New York; the state chairman, Michael J. Prendergast; and the national committeeman and party boss, Carmine De Sapio. The lineup in effect gave De Sapio two voices, as Prendergast was a figurehead whose role did not include contradicting the boss.

Occasionally Boss Buckley of the Bronx, or Boss Sharkey of Brooklyn, or Boss Crotty of Buffalo would wander in, seeking a progress report for their own delegations, which were growing restive for news and willing to settle for rumors. There wasn't any news. Harriman stood pat for Murray, De Sapio held to his position that the leaders around the state wanted no part of Murray and did want Hogan. Neither Finletter nor any dark-horse substitute was given consideration. Regular as clockwork Prendergast would suggest that the only compromise candidate possible was Mayor Wagner.

Each time his name was mentioned, the mayor sat silently. He had already counted off reasons why he was not interested. One was that he had given his pledge to the city voters the year before that he would serve out his full second term as mayor. Another was that he had run for the Senate in 1956 and for mayor in 1957 and that a third campaign in 1958 meant just that much more time away from his wife and children. Still a third reason involved the succession at City Hall if he left the mayoralty.

The man who would inherit temporarily and would probably insist on nomination at a special election to fill out the balance of the Wagner term, was Abe Stark, president of the City Council. While Stark had many friends, there were even more who felt that he did not measure up to the mayoralty. He would be the city's first Jewish mayor, and a large segment of the upper crust of the Jewish community did not regard him as properly representative. In the Catholic community some did not want a Jewish mayor at all. Both groups were fully capable of voting against Wagner for senator just to keep Stark out of the mayoralty.

Eventually it was Averell Harriman who turned to Wagner and asked him to make the race anyhow, in the interest of party unity. If Wagner's answer had been affirmative, it would have been supported by De Sapio.

Instead, the mayor for the first time contributed the overweening reason why he would not make the race—his injured pride. He looked the governor coldly in the eye, and said, "You didn't want me on the ticket three months ago. I don't see how you need me now." And he got up to go, to join his wife and two sons who were on a sightseeing tour of Niagara Falls, a dozen miles away. Before he left, he was persuaded to think the matter over again and to meet with Harriman for breakfast the following (Tuesday) morning. But Wagner made it clear there was no real chance he would change his mind.

The exchange broke up the conference, and the decision on the Senate seat was put off to the next day. But Harriman consented to being nominated himself that night. Then, and only then, did De Sapio pass the word to the Brooklyn leader to caucus his delegation and come out for Hogan. This was the irrevocable step De Sapio had held off taking, and he couldn't have taken it until (1) Wagner was out of the picture and (2) Harriman had consented to run regardless of the identity of his running mates, which decision was inherent in Harriman's Monday-night acceptance speech.

Up to then, Harriman could have forced the nomination of Murray by refusing to run for governor unless he could pick his running mates. It would have placed the party leadership in an impossible light, and the opposition to Murray would have been forced to fold.

Al Smith had used that weapon in 1922, refusing to accept nomination for a second term as governor unless he had positive assurance that William Randolph Hearst would *not* be on the ticket with him. He won his point. In 1938 Herbert Lehman had used the same tactics, refusing to yield to a draft for a fourth term as governor unless he had his own choice, Charles Poletti, for lieutenant governor. And Lehman had his way.

Tuesday morning, over the breakfast table, Wagner reiterated to

Harriman his refusal to make the race. The afternoon brought the final meeting of Harriman, Wagner, De Sapio, and Prendergast. De Sapio insisted that he and the other leaders could not be for Murray, but stuck to the story that he personally had no candidate. In this he was less than ingenuous. Boss Sharkey of Brooklyn, on a signal from De Sapio, had already held a caucus of the Kings County delegation, which at his direction had voted unanimously for Hogan. Wagner reminded De Sapio that Buckley had been proselytizing for Hogan in De Sapio's behalf all during the past weekend, and the boss smiled wanly.

Harriman turned to him and said, "You are my secretary of state, my appointee. I want you to be with me." "I can't," said De Sapio, without elaboration. And that was that.

Harriman's aides made the last-minute contacts with the county chairmen who had decided to stick with the governor; De Sapio's allies passed the word to their own followers that the showdown was to be on the convention floor. It was after midnight before the long roll was completed. The final score was Hogan 772, Murray 304, and Finletter 66. The bulk of the Hogan votes came from New York, Bronx, Kings, Queens, Richmond, Erie, Oneida, Onondaga, and Suffolk counties; the Murray votes were gleaned from Westchester, Albany, Monroe, and a scattering of smaller upstate counties. Finletter got twenty-one of his votes from the Manhattan Reform clubs and the balance from Nassau County, whose boss, John F. English, delighted in the role of party maverick.

The rout of the Harriman forces was completed by the nomination of Peter Crotty, the Erie County boss, for attorney general, the other vacancy on the ticket. The Crotty nomination added to the picture of boss domination and served to confirm what the reporters suspected, but did not actually know. The press coverage concentrated on the rule of the boss; it pictured De Sapio as insisting on Hogan with no compromise possible, overriding the wishes of both Harriman and Wagner. The reporters had no knowledge of Harriman's rejection of Wagner months earlier—Wagner's real reason for refusing to accept when Harriman finally turned so desperately to him.

Throughout the conferences Wagner had been mildly sympathetic to the idea that Harriman, as the man running for reelection as governor, should have been deferred to on the picking of his running mates, but he did not feel it incumbent on him to use his own patronage hold on De Sapio's machine to demand that action. He was even a little inwardly pleased with the turn of events that made Harriman ask him for help by running with him, and that he had stood firm on his refusal. Nobody at that point really felt that the election had been lost. In fact, Harriman and his staff remained supremely confident throughout the campaign. De Sapio, more realistic, moved to bring unity behind the Harriman-Hogan ticket by naming Tom Finletter chairman of the campaign committee.

Finletter had already been nominated for senator by the Liberal Party, whose convention met at the same time as the Democrats', a move which reflected the hopes of Backer and Alex Rose that the Democrats would also nominate Harriman's "second choice." Finletter withdrew the next day. Wagner was given the assignment of persuading Herbert Lehman to endorse Hogan and to use his extensive influence with the Liberal Party to get them to substitute Hogan as their nominee. Wagner telephoned Lehman, who was vacationing in Switzerland. He had been kept in touch with the Buffalo developments by his own aide, Julius C. C. Edelstein, who doubled in brass as Finletter's political activist.

Lehman agreed to release a telegram to Alex Rose, reading: "Although shocked and deeply distressed by what happened in Buffalo, greatly hope Liberal Party will endorse Hogan, Regards."

Lehman's blessing of the Hogan nomination was vital. He had standing with the voters that was second to none. While he never aroused their personal enthusiasm the way Al Smith had done a generation before, his hold on the electorate was just as firm. Lehman himself was a social-minded ex-banker with a long record of quiet philanthropy. He was intensely serious, almost to the point of being humorless. He had a deep-seated feeling about the office of governor, which he had held for a full decade. He believed that the office itself was entitled to respect, regardless of its occupant.

By Lehman's standards, De Sapio's refusal to yield to Harriman's requests had demeaned the office of governor and thereby reflected on all who had held it, including himself. The depth of this feeling he was to demonstrate shortly. But for the moment he endorsed Hogan, whom he did regard as qualified for the Senate, and persuaded the Liberal Party to go along.

The Liberal Party alliance with the Democrats was traditional in state campaigns in that era, and thus its endorsement of the Harriman-Hogan ticket did not increase the vote potential, although without it the ticket would have been doomed. As things were, Harriman in particular faced tough going against an unusually attractive Republican nominee for governor in the person of Nelson Rockefeller.

Prior to his nomination, Rockefeller had been known principally as just one of the five grandsons of the original John D. Rockefeller, the hard-bitten accumulator of America's greatest fortune. John D. Rockefeller, Jr., had devoted his life to giving back, via philanthropy and foundations, a substantial portion of the income the founder's estate had guaranteed. Nelson, in the third generation, was the first Rockefeller to turn to politics as a career. He had attracted a mild amount of public attention when he served in Franklin Roosevelt's administration as Coordinator of Latin-American Affairs and later as a roving Assistant Secretary of State in the Eisenhower administration. He was not clearly identified as a Republican in the eyes of the New York voters prior to his nomination.

Averell Harriman had given Rockefeller something of a springboard in the state by naming him head of a commission to develop data and background materials—an agenda—for a state constitutional convention. But the convention itself never materialized, and in the winter of 1957–58, the season when the conception of candidates occurs, there were few who were thinking in terms of Nelson Rockefeller as the Republican nominee for governor. The exceptions were Rockefeller himself and the few he had sounded out as to his prospects.

Harriman himself gave Rockefeller the first nod of recognition as his probable rival, under circumstances that gave Rockefeller advertising among the groups in which he needed it the most—the professional politicians, the political reporters, and the editorial writers. It happened in March, at the annual dinner in Albany of the

New York State Legislative Correspondents Association, the state version of the Washington Gridiron Club stunt dinner. Each year since 1900 the Capitol reporters had put on a show spoofing the politicians and the political scene, and giving the governor the right to hit back at the final curtain. Reporting of speeches made at the dinner was always forbidden, but this did not stop political history from being made.

In 1908 Governor Charles Evans Hughes, his pink whiskers seemingly aflame with indignation, stormed up and down the room, denouncing to their faces the political bosses of his own Republican Party. In 1939 Tom Dewey used the occasion to tell the 340 elite dinner guests that he was discarding the man who had made him politically, the national committeeman Kenneth F. Simpson. Three years later Wendell L. Willkie, the party's most recent presidential nominee, ruled out the same Tom Dewey from consideration as the party's nominee for governor or for President. Dewey, present, sat silently, knowing that he, not Willkie, controlled the party in the state.

At the 1958 show the reporters on stage impersonated the men they thought were potential Republican nominees for governor, exposed their frailties, real or imagined, and predicted in song and dialogue the rout of any one of them by the incumbent Harriman. In the last estimate they were on safe ground. No incumbent governor seeking reelection had been defeated since Nathan L. Miller had been beaten by Al Smith in 1922, and even in that case, Smith had a prior record of incumbency equal to Miller's.

As Harriman rose to make the traditional reply closing the show, he recalled that the reporters had listed Assembly Speaker Oswald D. Heck, Senate Majority Leader Walter J. Mahoney, Republican National Chairman Leonard Hall, and U.S. Attorney Paul W. Williams as his possible opponents. "But you left out the most likely of all, Nelson Rockefeller," said Harriman. Turning to a man seated at his own head table, unrecognized by most in the room, he added, "Stand up and take a bow, Nelson."

Rockefeller did. It was his inaugural as a candidate for elective office.

Harriman's motivation in thus publicizing a potentially danger-ous opponent was never clarified. It is possible that he had detected a swell for Rockefeller in the banking community, in which both had been raised, and felt that by exposing the still underground Rockefeller candidacy to the light of day he would weaken it. Pos-sibly he was so confident of his own political appeal that he preferred to run and win against a Rockefeller—America's best-known name—than some run-of-the-mill nominee.

What he succeeded in doing was to make the Rockefeller nomi-nation a possibility for the first time in the minds of the political reporters and political leaders to whom it had not yet occurred. From then on, Rockefeller's name figured in the news stories reporting or speculating on the gubernatorial prospects.

Months went by and as the convention neared, Messrs. Heck, Mahoney, Hall, and Williams one by one concluded that attempting to block the possessor of so much of the Rockefeller fortune was equivalent to halting a fast freight by lying down on the tracks. In seeking his first nomination, Rockefeller did not blitz his way into the public consciousness by TV commercials or newspaper advertis-ing. He won it by "persuading" every other possible contender to withdraw. The persuasion was hidden, but powerful. Those who had counted on running suddenly found normal sources of campaign financing unavailable to them. County chairmen on whose support they had counted responded instead to pressure from the Rockefeller forces.

The word that Rockefeller was the man to support flowed from the banking community to the business community, affecting even the home towns of the other contenders. And business support has always been a large factor in the determination of Republican nomi-nations.

None of the other potential nominees took the onward rush of the newcomer happily. They privately resented the fact that their records of public and party service meant nothing in the face of the Rockefeller fortune. Leonard Hall in particular rebelled. He pulled out of the state picture entirely, and later used his widespread national contacts to oppose Rockefeller's presidential aspirations both in 1960 and 1964. It was years before he was eventually reconciled.

By the time the convention met there was nothing left for it to do on the governorship but ratify the only name presented to it, which it did with enthusiasm, since Rockefeller's was definitely the freshest face around. There was not even the formality of a roll call. Yet essentially the convention which nominated Rockefeller was the most boss-ridden in party history. The difference between it and the Democratic conclave in Buffalo was that the Republican boss was not there, in fact, was not even a human being.

In the picking of a candidate for U.S. senator, a real live boss did figure. He was J. Russel Sprague, once the state boss, now reduced to Nassau County jurisdiction. The convention, left to its own devices, would have nominated Joseph Carlino of Nassau, the popular majority leader of the state assembly, for the Senate. However, Carlino was about to be promoted to assembly speaker to succeed the retiring Oswald Heck, and Sprague preferred this sure hold on the top legislative post. He vetoed Carlino for senator, and the delegates wound up selecting a middle-of-the-road congressman from Rochester, Kenneth B. Keating.

Keating was then unknown in the rest of the state. He made up for it during the campaign by a record hand-shaking tour which carried him into every city ghetto and every rural hamlet.

But it was Rockefeller who stole the show. His first campaign for governor was his best-run, most splendid performance. He was then an exceptionally vigorous fifty-year-old who acted as though every moment on the stump, every tour through the hustings, was what he had been waiting for all his luxurious life. With his gesture of draping an arm around the nearest well-wisher and saying "H'are ya, fella?" Rockefeller looked particularly warm in contrast with the stiffer, more formal Harriman. "Rocky," as he was immediately dubbed, ate hot dogs on the Coney Island boardwalk, consumed blintzes on the lower East Side, chewed pizza with the Italians, turning what had once been an occasional accommodation to group habits into a permanent campaign ritual.

When it came to the issues, he charged Harriman with having plunged the state into debt with little or nothing to show for the money that had been spent. He pledged a pay-as-you-go fiscal policy (which he scrapped in short order as governor when he found it did not meet state needs) and outlined a vast program of public improvements, which, he said, had been neglected in the Harriman administration.

Actually Harriman had been an adequate governor—he might even have been hailed as a great governor in some state with a less demanding tradition. His weakness lay in his failure to identify with the voters, either personally or as the promoter of program or principle. Even his speechwriters found difficulty in synthesizing his candidacy. His name was well known, but his opponent's outmatched it.

On the stump Harriman seemed to think that shaking hands with any passerby was a vote-getting tactic. Rockefeller went after the ethnic blocs, and no bloc was too small for him to court and for his brilliantly organized campaign staff to pursue. For example, riding the ferry to Staten Island for a day's campaigning there, Rockefeller had his shoes shined by the Italian bootblack who worked the beat. Two days later the bootblack received at his home a personal note and a picture of Rockefeller autographed to "my good friend Tony." The note hailed the shoeshine as the best Rockefeller had ever had, and the candidate inquired whether Tony could possibly be available for a repeat performance on a scheduled return trip to Staten Island the following week. More than Tony's vote was involved. The incident was spread by Tony and his family throughout the close-knit Italian community, which furnished more than 40 percent of the Staten Island vote.

Rockefeller developed amazing support in the New York City Jewish community, normally heavily Democratic and expected to be solidly in Harriman's corner because of his New Deal identification. Instead, there developed a sort of inverse snob appeal, which induced many of the city's Jews to feel that they themselves were somehow richer by being able to patronize a Rockefeller, to do a favor for the world's richest family by voting for one of its sons. In the face of that defection Harriman was able on election day to mount a city majority

157

of only 310,000, far short of what was needed. Rockefeller, on the other hand, swept upstate, to get a resounding overall majority of 573,000.

Hogan, who was the butt of anti-boss campaign propaganda, fared far better than Harriman both upstate and down, against the admittedly weaker Keating. He carried New York City by 594,000 votes but lost the election statewide by 133,000.

Hogan would have done better, could even have won, if his campaign had not been sabotaged in his own headquarters and at the polls by the reformers. De Sapio, in his eagerness to heal party wounds, had turned over the actual management of the Harriman-Hogan joint campaign to the reformers when he appointed Finletter chairman of the Citizens Committee for Harriman-Hogan. Finletter recruited his top aides from the reform movement, and some of them operated more in the interest of developing reform than in electing Hogan as senator. This author, working at Hogan headquarters, noted instances where organization-minded workers were detached from the campaign payroll as soon as their political orientation became clear; where campaign literature paid for by the committee was slanted toward maximizing rather than minimizing the boss issue; where Hogan's campaign was kept from a speedy take-off by the holding back from the candidate of speeches written for his consideration and delivery.

The result of the petty sniping was a campaign that was slow in starting, that lacked luster throughout, that underplayed the nominee's previous record in office, and that failed to establish for him any qualifications for higher office.

In a graceful speech to his personal staff on election night, after the polls had told their sad story, Hogan stressed that he was not upset; that he truly enjoyed the job he had; that he would still be district attorney as the unanimous choice of all the parties; and that he could continue as such without ever again having to wage a campaign contest. If he really did draw such comfort from the results, he was the only one who did.

TEN

THE REFORM ARMY RALLIES

The Buffalo convention and the election defeat that followed it turned the hitherto straggling and disunited reform movement into an organized army marching on De Sapio. The man responsible for the new impetus was the eighty-one-year-old Herbert Lehman, still smarting over De Sapio's denigration of the governorship. Lehman's contribution to De Sapio's political demise overshadowed that of Eleanor Roosevelt, the illustrious former first lady of the land, who shared with Lehman the titular command of the anti–De Sapio forces.

Up to Lehman's taking charge, the reform movement consisted of half a dozen political clubs scattered through Manhattan. It did not exist in the other four boroughs. Most of its membership was self-recruited, reflecting the yen of upper-middle-class Democrats for the political participation that had been denied to them by the regular organization clubs.

Some of the groups stood committed to reform for the sake of better candidates for public office and better district leaders in party office; some were committed to reform just for the sake of a banner under which to march; others joined up in behalf of a possible third presidential bid for Adlai Stevenson, which, they felt, would not be aided by the party regulars. These divisions of purpose existed not only among the clubs but within the clubs, so that they seldom presented a united front on any issue. Only in Village Independent Democrats, the maverick of mavericks, was there unity of purpose—the ousting of De Sapio—which was the natural result of its having been formed to contest the control of De Sapio's own Tamawa Club.

In the light of the highly publicized reform disunity, it was hard for De Sapio to take the reform movement seriously. He greeted allusions to it with a horselaugh and went his own way preaching the virtues of political reform and voter participation, contending that his organized approach was the effective one, contrasted with the chaos so apparent in the opposition.

George Backer, while still functioning as an unsalaried Harriman brain-truster, made the first feeble attempt to unite the reformers against De Sapio. He was so upset by the refusal of the Buffalo delegates to take Finletter's senatorial candidacy seriously that he moved without waiting for the gubernatorial campaign to get under way. He set up the Council of Reform Democrats and solicited Lehman's support for an immediate drive to oust De Sapio. He ran into the argument that no overt action should be taken until after the election, lest the reform movement be blamed for defeat if it materialized.

After the election Lehman made his move, with his own rather than Backer's organization. After weeks of quiet preparation a press conference was held on January 22, 1959, to announce the formation of a new central reform organization. Entitled the Committee for Democratic Voters (CDV), it set up permanent headquarters at 120 East 56th Street, under the guidance of a triumvirate consisting of Lehman, Mrs. Roosevelt, and Finletter.

The pronunciamento they issued that day called for a democratization of party procedures to destroy the "image of bossism" which had handicapped the party. Noting Democratic victories in other parts of the nation, whereas the New York ticket had been defeated, they argued that "in New York the party remains in the hands of the old-style party professionals" and that "public confidence in the quality, integrity, and direction of the leadership has been disastrously impaired, as was clearly shown in the election in November."

Nowhere in the statement was there mention of De Sapio by name. They had painstakingly hammered out in their strategy talks an agreement that the reform target should not be personalized.

They agreed that De Sapio was both persuasive and popular, so that hitting at him rather than at the general need for new leadership could weaken their cause. In a trial run of the press conference, Paul Bragdon, executive director of the CDV, threw at the three principals the hard questions they could expect from the press, and the rehearsed answers carefully skirted any direct attack on the boss.

Lehman cast that discretion to the winds at the actual press conference an hour later. Pinpointing De Sapio as the target, he said, "I think that Mr. De Sapio gave the Republicans a made-to-order issue of bossism. We will oppose Mr. De Sapio and hope that the voters will take the steps to remove him."

Lehman's directness made the headlines. It also made De Sapio aware that he now had a formidable opponent, one whose reputation was such that his motivation was difficult to challenge; and one who stood high in the regard of the mayor, with whom his own leadership was so closely tied. De Sapio swore to himself, but publicly gave the soft answer that was typical when he felt that the time had not come for hitting hard: "I sincerely regret that Senator Lehman has seen fit to engage in personalities. The Democratic Party and the principles it represents is above that. No one individual is more important than his party."

Mrs. Roosevelt's heavy speaking schedule and other commitments barred her from full-time participation in the reform movement. Finletter did not have the prestige of either of the others. So Lehman became the "operational" member, functioning through his senatorial administrative assistant, Julius C. C. Edelstein, who spoke in the senator's name on day-to-day operations and strategy decisions. With Lehman's help the CDV raised $500,000, which it spent over a five-year period in its drive to beat De Sapio and in its later unsuccessful effort to take over Tammany Hall. Additional funds, characterized politically as "Stevenson money," were poured in by Adele Levy and J. M. Kaplan, wealthy philanthropists, for the purpose of defeating De Sapio in his home assembly district in Greenwich Village.

Within the Democratic Party in Manhattan the choice of being for or against De Sapio obliterated most of the reform distinctions based on ideology. Inevitably as both sides pressed toward the 1959 primary, the language grew rougher, the tactics tougher. Sydney Baron had only a loose checkrein as De Sapio's statement writer, and Edelstein punched as hard as he wanted for Lehman.

The 1959 primary was the first one waged on a county-wide scale since De Sapio had forced through the direct election system. Its results demonstrated the impressive potential of a united reform movement. In the fight for election of county committeemen, De Sapio's forces won 1,900 seats against 900 for the reformers. An additional 400 were the property of a Harlem-based offshoot of the regular machine, led by the controversial black congressman Adam Clayton Powell. Powell had supported Dwight Eisenhower for President in 1956, and De Sapio, in reprisal, had sponsored a rival candidate in the Democratic primary that same year. So Powell withdrew his bloc from De Sapio, but did not bolster the reform movement.

The primary produced a roughly parallel division of strength inside the Tammany executive committee. It reelected De Sapio leader by a vote of ten for and six against. Of the six, 3½ votes represented reform strength, and 2½ Powell's blacks.

The most threatening vote had been in Greenwich Village, the base on which rested De Sapio's whole political pyramid. His position as de facto leader of his party in the city and the state stemmed from his leadership of Tammany Hall. That leadership in turn rested on his district leadership, for under Tammany's rule only a district leader could be county leader. And the district leadership depended on a popular majority within the district itself. In the challenge for that vital base, De Sapio won in 1959 by a vote of only 4,857 to 4,271. His opponent, Charles McGuinness, a thirty-one-year-old lawyer with no previous record of political activity, ran under the emblem of the Village Independent Democrats.

De Sapio's strength was still as great in Little Italy, but the district included less of that territory and more of the high-rental apartment houses on lower Fifth Avenue and elegant townhouses on the side streets. The political boundaries had been changed since the days when young Carmine De Sapio first challenged Sheriff Dan Finn, and even within the retained areas there were fewer voters with strong organizational ties.

162

De Sapio had the majority in the Tammany executive committee, which could have waived the requirement that the county leader be a district leader. It had been waived once before. He also had the votes in the membership of the First Assembly District county committee, controlled by the Tamawa Club, to turn his district leadership over to some trusted lieutenant, removing himself as an easy target. Some of his friends advised him to do one or both.

He recognized the danger, but couldn't bring himself to protect himself that way. The closeness of the popular vote made it too late for him to retire gracefully from Village politics while retaining his other leaderships, and he was too proud to step aside while under fire. He recalled his own words to the executive committee when he forced through the system for the direct election of its members, that any man who couldn't carry his own district under his own name should not aspire to leadership.

He made more frequent appearances at the Tamawa Club, but to the voters of lower Fifth Avenue he was just the tall man in dark glasses who hailed a taxicab going uptown around 10:30 every morning and might be seen emerging from one near midnight on his return home. He was free of the duties of public office—light as they had been as either a member of the Board of Elections or secretary of state—but he carried a heavy schedule in his office at the Hotel Biltmore. He took very seriously his position as national committeeman, spokesman for his state on national politics. The 1960 national convention was in the offing, and it would pick a nominee for President who could be a winner, now that the amendment barring a third term was operating for the first time against an incumbent, Dwight D. Eisenhower.

Neither De Sapio nor anyone else foresaw that the presidential politics of 1960 would weaken rather than strengthen his reputation for political sagacity and would be an important factor in creating the first breach between him and Mayor Wagner.

After the formation of the CDV there was no immediate change in the Wagner–De Sapio relationship. Wagner had no desire to alienate himself from Lehman and Mrs. Roosevelt, but neither did he want to drop the political agent who took so many chores off his own hands and carried them out so well. Wagner still appreciated

163

how easy it was to deal with De Sapio, compared with other leaders.

At Tammany's annual dinner early in 1959 Wagner, after mulling over more than usual the language of his speech, reiterated his previous evaluation of De Sapio as the best leader the party had ever had. At a state committee fund-raising dinner that same banquet season, Wagner defended the essential democracy of the Buffalo convention. He noted that its choices had been made by the delegates on an open roll call, whereas at the Republican convention the selection was narrowed in advance to one candidate, as the result of underground financial pressures.

Mike Prendergast, the Democratic state chairman, was unhesitatingly 110 percent loyal to De Sapio. Prendergast's predecessor, Richard H. Balch of Utica, had quit the job years before because he felt that the state chairman was just a dummy as long as De Sapio was the real boss. De Sapio had hand-picked Prendergast, chairman of Governor Harriman's home county of Rockland, as Balch's successor. Up to then the new chairman had been a small-time operator even in his home county, and now he enjoyed the statewide spotlight, even though his duties involved just being De Sapio's echo. He soon turned into a more vigorous and outspoken advocate of the boss than De Sapio could have been on his own. Thus when it came time for the state committee to pick the elite list of party dignitaries who would go to the national convention as delegates-at-large, Prendergast decided that Lehman, avowed enemy of the boss, should not be included.

That kind of slap at a man who had been so often the party's standard-bearer was unprecedented. In the middle 1930s Al Smith was the leading Democrat opposed to Franklin Roosevelt and his New Deal. Yet Jim Farley, Roosevelt's agent, still honored Smith's standing in the party by picking him as delegate-at-large to the 1936 convention, committed in advance to renominating Roosevelt by acclamation for a second term. That Smith declined (he announced he would be "taking a walk" at convention time) was not relevant. Farley knew that the personal predilections of just one delegate out of a hundred-odd should not be stacked up against the number of important people who would have resented the dropping of Smith. But Prendergast's perspective was narrower than Farley's.

The calculated snub of Lehman was more than Mayor Wagner could stomach. He first considered showing his displeasure by boycotting the meeting at which the Prendergast slate would be adopted. Then he decided on a more forceful approach; Wagner had already been named as titular chairman of the state delegation.

He drove up to Albany for the state committee session and told De Sapio and Prendergast—privately, he thought—that he would call for a volunteer to resign from the delegation to make room for Lehman, and that as delegation chairman he would then appoint Lehman to the vacancy, regardless of rules or fine points of procedure. De Sapio, who had backed Prendergast initially, was aghast at that kind of confrontation with the mayor, on an issue that was basically petty and pointless. He suggested to Prendergast the only graceful way out: that Prendergast himself should resign from the delegation and Lehman would be elected in his stead. Prendergast agreed, but under protest. The press might never have known what had gone on except that by chance a United Press reporter rode the same hotel elevator as Wagner, De Sapio, and Prendergast and heard them battling it out. The story went out on the wire-service lines while the three men were still ironing out details of a settlement.

It was the first time in their relationship of more than a decade that Wagner and De Sapio came to anything approaching a showdown. The seed of disunity was planted. It went on to flourish as the boss and the mayor pursued separate and potentially conflicting personal interests in the hot climate of presidential-year politics.

De Sapio's ambition was to be the President-maker in 1960. He had his choice of two routes toward that goal. One was to identify himself early with the man who would turn out to be the convention winner, so that there would be an established warm relationship when the candidate became President. The second path called for holding back his own support—and New York State's 114 votes, the largest bloc in the country—until the convention had taken a ballot or two, thus creating the winner by either throwing him New York's bloc at the moment it represented the votes needed for nomination or starting a bandwagon movement that would achieve the same result.

De Sapio elected to travel the second path, which gave him more time for decision, more room for maneuvers. He had looked over the Democratic hopefuls—John F. Kennedy of Massachusetts, Hubert Humphrey of Minnesota, Stuart Symington of Missouri, Lyndon Johnson of Texas, as well as the possibility of Adlai Stevenson—and did not identify any one of them as a sure winner. There would be time at the convention itself.

He could not visualize a third nomination for Stevenson, even though he knew that big names, with loud voices, in the New York establishment would demand it. He foresaw the possibility of Kennedy and Humphrey fighting it out in the primaries, and guessed they might eliminate themselves by failing to establish widespread popularity. Johnson of Texas—well, no Southerner had been nominated since the Civil War. He was intrigued with the possibility of Stuart Symington, who had the backing of former President Truman and was the most likely to attract support from the big party organizations in the industrial states. For De Sapio envisioned the nomination being made by the bosses of the big machines, of which he was a leader, and he never questioned his ability to deliver the New York votes when the time was ripe.

Mayor Wagner, independent of the considerations that influenced De Sapio, nursed vice-presidential ambitions, which, of course, hinged on who was nominated for President. A ticket of Kennedy and Wagner was impossible, since both were Catholics. A ticket with either Stevenson or Humphrey at its head was unlikely, so Wagner dealt behind the scenes with Lyndon Johnson, certain that if Johnson were the nominee, the balancing of the ticket would call for a prominent Eastern Catholic for second place.

Both Wagner and De Sapio underestimated the finesse as well as the power of the Kennedy clan. John M. Bailey of Connecticut, the Kennedy agent for dealing with most of the professional politicians, surreptitiously rounded up substantial Kennedy support in upstate New York without De Sapio's ever hearing that Bailey had crossed the state line. Bailey's negotiations were aided by the special appeal

166

the Kennedy candidacy had to the Irish political leadership, which still ruled the roost in many non-Irish communities. Joseph P. Kennedy, the founding father, used the personal relationship he had with Buckley, the Bronx boss—they had been next-door neighbors in Riverdale—to detach the Bronx delegation from any possible De Sapio coalition and ally it with the Kennedy fortunes. The elder Kennedy also was able to influence Peter Crotty of Buffalo, the O'Connells in Albany, John English in Nassau, and Congressman Eugene J. Keogh, the real activist behind the Brooklyn machine.

De Sapio's program for control of the state delegation, which he had had in mind in the 1958 battle to show who was boss, was dead before he even got around to canvassing his supporters. His plan for trading with a yet-to-be-selected contender at the convention was defeated in his own backyard by the old political axiom that it is impossible to beat somebody with nobody. The result was that he had no alternative but to throw the New York votes—except for those of the die-hard Stevenson supporters from the reform districts—to the Kennedy candidacy a few weeks before the convention. He thus missed both paths to glory—picking the winner early, or furnishing the votes to put him over.

The Kennedys accepted the De Sapio support without any feeling of deep obligation, for they knew the New York score. Wagner's vice-presidential aspirations disappeared at the same time without a trace. In the weeks that followed the nomination of John F. Kennedy for President, De Sapio, Wagner, and the New York reform movement patched together an uneasy truce to work for the victory of the Kennedy-Johnson ticket. The principal gluing element was the dislike of all of them for the Republican ticket of Nixon and Lodge.

How tenuous was the alliance became evident when John F. Kennedy came to New York in the midst of a whirlwind campaign the week before election, to address the major rally that Prendergast and De Sapio had arranged to be held in Columbus Circle. On his arrival Kennedy learned that both Herbert Lehman and Eleanor Roosevelt had declined to attend if they were to be limited to the role of dressing up the dais. If they came, they said, it would be as scheduled speakers, or else they would not come at all. Kennedy wanted them there, not only for their prestige but for their identification as leaders of the Stevenson wing of the party. He picked up the telephone and called De Sapio. He explained what he wanted.

"I'll see what I can do," said De Sapio, meaning that he would go along with the Kennedy request. Then he added, "It would be helpful if you talked to Mike, too."

So the tired, travel-worn nominee called Prendergast, only to find him stubbornly opposed to any sort of recognition of Lehman and Mrs. Roosevelt. Kennedy, in a role strange to him, pleaded, several times reminding the grudge-bearing state chairman that it was the presidential nominee who was personally asking the favor. Eventually, convinced that he had obtained Prendergast's assent, he said, "Thanks a lot, Mike. I knew you'd understand how important it is to me."

Kennedy arrived at Columbus Circle hours later, just in time to deliver his speech over a nationwide TV network. As he finished it and went off the air, he was confronted by Herbert Lehman, white with indignation, who declared that he had been "double-crossed."

"You mean you weren't allowed to speak?" asked Kennedy. Lehman nodded. "You weren't double-crossed," said Kennedy. "I was. And I'll get the dirty son of a bitch bastard who did it if it's the last thing I do."

He meant Prendergast, who, he felt, was responsible. And after his election he did not forget. He sent John Bailey to see De Sapio, demanding Prendergast's head. Bailey said that the incoming administration was willing to give De Sapio full recognition as national committeeman—which meant control of patronage—only if Prendergast was dropped as state chairman. De Sapio, loyal to his supporter, declined to make the commitment.

The Kennedy administration, tolerant of big-city machines all over the country, was not thereafter hostile to De Sapio, but neither did it take the steps to bolster De Sapio's leadership which it otherwise might have done. And now De Sapio really needed help.

On election night itself, after the votes in New York had been counted, Herbert Lehman took to the airwaves to renew the anti–De Sapio drive. He declared that the pre-election truce had ended and that the De Sapio rule of New York must be terminated for the sake of the legislative program of the incoming Kennedy administration.

De Sapio's reply the next day was bitter. Sydney Baron put it into form, but it reflected De Sapio's own indignation:

The so-called insurgents piously declared last night that our state would not be able to support Senator Kennedy's program unless the party leadership here is changed.

The apparent hypocrisy of this assertion is demonstrated by the election results and gains in New York and by the fact that Senator Lehman was probably the most active and impassioned man at the convention in Los Angeles in opposition to the nomination of Senator Kennedy. He repeatedly raised his tired old cry of bossism and accused the delegation who represented and gave 104½ votes to Senator Kennedy of being boss-controlled. He predicted that "we would regret the day that Kennedy was nominated."

The time has come to stop coddling those who, resting on past laurels, resort to deceit and demagoguery as they permit themselves to be used by opportunists who desire to ruin the Democratic Party. They will neither rule nor ruin the party, and if it is a "war" they want, they shall have it.

The people will not be fooled by false and sanctimonious claims and charges. They know that if anyone or any group has the moral and practical right to call itself reform, it is the present leadership of the New York County Democratic organization.

We have fought for and achieved virtually every reform which has been advocated and sought by our responsible civic groups. One important reform remains unattained—that is, reforming the sham and exposing the selfish, divisive activities of a small group of self-proclaimed prophets who themselves want nothing less than to be bosses.

Wagner realized that the war had indeed begun. With the mayoralty election of 1961 next on the political calendar, he was involved, whether he liked it or not, whether he sought a third term for himself or operated to secure the job for a hand-picked successor. He would have to choose soon between Senator Lehman and Mrs. Roosevelt, whom he had always courted, and De Sapio, the political leader he admired and valued.

In his comment to the press on the De Sapio–Lehman controversy, the mayor said simply, "As the leader of the Democratic

Party in the City of New York, I will have a great deal to say about the future of the party here. I am going to really assert that leadership." It was Wagner's first public avowal of the right of the mayor to be the party leader, and as such it denigrated De Sapio.

Wagner had been particularly impressed with a result in the September primary contest for Congress on the middle West Side, strong Democratic territory in which the mayor himself had always run well. In the primary Ludwig Teller, the incumbent, who was the organization choice for renomination and the possessor of a respectable record in Congress, had been defeated by William Fitts Ryan, reformer. The Ryan forces used the device of simply pasting a sticker under Teller's name on his campaign posters, identifying him as "De Sapio's candidate." The reformers converted De Sapio's name into an epithet, and won the primary on the basis of that alone.

The mayor revealed his thinking in midwinter at a conference of his close aides in the drawing room of Gracie Mansion. The subject of the conference was the mayoralty campaign of 1961: what kind of campaign should be projected in the event the mayor decided to run again. Wagner, as was his habit, just listened throughout the discussion. He interrupted just once, saying, "After what happened to Lou Teller, what I want to know is how anyone can win if he has De Sapio's support."

It was his first signal to his aides that he had made up his mind to end his political marriage with De Sapio; that he had decided that if he himself was to survive politically he had to break off with the man who had made him.

ELEVEN

THE DOWNHILL ROAD

The decision of Bob Wagner to sever the political bonds which held him to De Sapio was the turning point in the boss's career. The loss of the governorship in the 1958 election was not too disastrous; the leverage that City Hall could exert against him was. Once Wagner moved to implement his policy of self-protection, De Sapio's political progress was all downgrade, at a rate of descent many times faster than his original, painstaking climb to the heights.

Wagner was not crude. He embarked on no housecleaning of city aides who had been recommended to him by De Sapio. Such a course would have reflected on his own previous acceptance of De Sapio as political employment agent and would, besides, have hurt a lot of small people. But the mayor did pass the word that future preference at City Hall would be banned for De Sapio supporters, and instead would rest with those reform clubs which were interested. What hurt De Sapio particularly was that he could no longer present names of prospective judges, whom the mayor had the power to appoint.

De Sapio now had working against him, in addition to the patronage controls of the mayor's office, the very political reforms he himself had instituted, particularly the direct election of Tammany's district leaders and the reduction of the county committee membership to a workable number. The result was that in the first nine months of 1961 he lost all of his political positions, with the exception of the Democratic national committee membership, in which post he was a lame duck finishing his term with no chance of re-election.

But De Sapio retained much that was personally gratifying. For example, the people of Little Italy, although by now a minority in a changing area, continued to vote for him as the Greenwich Village district leader as long as he presented his name on the ballot. He similarly kept the loyalty of a substantial bloc within the Tammany executive committee, although other members had gone down to defeat with him. He had many friends in the business community whom he had helped in their dealings with the city, and who did not choose to run away from him now that he had been defeated. As he walked the streets in midtown, or crossed the lobby of the Hotel Biltmore, he constantly encountered people in politics who had worked under him as boss and who still thought he had been The Best.

De Sapio remained convinced that he had been the victim of ingratitude and demagoguery, and he could not quite accept the triumph of injustice and the prospect of its continuance. Angry as he was at the mayor and the reformers, he still did not let that sour him on the rest of the world.

The series of events that resulted in De Sapio's political rout began in January of the 1961 mayoralty year. The first development was muted. Wagner detested personal confrontations on unpleasant subjects, so he saw to it that there never was one between himself and De Sapio. The mayor just cut off communications. De Sapio, after a few telephone calls which found the mayor "unavailable," was too proud to chase after his one-time partner. In addition, he soon learned, through the ever-functioning political grapevine, that the mayor had found a new political agent in Alex Rose, the leader of the Liberal Party.

Rose was a patient man who had been hoping for a key role in Wagner's political operations all through Wagner's first two terms, but had been in no position to press for it. He and his party had opposed Wagner's first bid for the mayoralty, so that if it had been up to Rose, Wagner would never have been mayor at all. But the Liberal Party boss had supported Wagner for the Senate in 1956 and for mayor in 1957, receiving in return a minuscule portion of city patronage. Wagner turned to him in 1961 because he needed a political agent to replace De Sapio; because Rose was a particularly shrewd political mechanic as well as strategist; and because Rose was persona grata with Lehman, Mrs. Roosevelt, and the reform elements in general.

De Sapio had sat across the dinner table from Rose on many occasions, in intimate conferences at which party nominations were exchanged, with Rose exercising full Liberal Party authority. The selection of Rose as his successor in the Wagner administration fanned De Sapio's resentment at being fired to conciliate the anti-boss brouhaha and the demand for greater public participation in party decision-making. He knew that the Liberal Party rules and practices under Rose's leadership were far less democratic than those De Sapio had installed in Tammany. "How hypocritical can you get?" De Sapio mused privately. For public consumption he contented himself, for the time, with saying:

"Tammany Hall for years has been unfairly stigmatized as something sinister and evil. But even those most outspoken in their attacks on Tammany Hall must admit it is immoral to visit the sins of the ancient past upon the New York County Democratic organization; upon the men and women who comprise it; and therefore the people and the programs it represents."

The extent of the alienation of Wagner from De Sapio became public knowledge in the course of the selection of a new borough president of Manhattan, the office that had led to their original alliance. Borough President Hulan E. Jack, whom both Wagner and De Sapio had sponsored as Wagner's successor, had proved a disappointment to both. Jack had run a lackluster, patronage-oriented shop for eight years, reflecting no credit on his own black community. Then he was foolish enough to allow a real-estate promoter who was seeking a city contract to refurbish, free of charge, his Harlem apartment. Jack forfeited his office when this was exposed. Under the city charter, his successor had to be picked by the Manhattan members of the City Council, five Democrats and one Republican.

Whereas only a few months earlier Wagner and De Sapio would have settled at the Gracie Mansion breakfast table how the councilmen would be told to vote, now each had his own candidate, and there was much political browbeating and arm twisting of the council members behind the scenes. Finally there was a public convocation of the councilmen, presided over by Wagner, at which the mayor's man won, four to two. De Sapio insinuated, and with reason, that Wagner had used his city commissioner of investigation, Louis Kaplan, to "persuade" two council members to switch their votes.

This defeat was more than De Sapio could take without reacting. He determined to stage a full-scale counterattack on the reform movement: he announced he would put nominees in the field in the fall primary against every reform district leader. If he was going to go down, he would go down fighting. Wagner's response was a public call—the mayor's first—for De Sapio's ouster as leader of Tammany Hall.

Wagner did so without embracing the reform movement. The mayor had no intention of turning party control over to a crew that he regarded, at the level below Lehman and Mrs. Roosevelt, as erratic and irresponsible, and not really in his own corner. He did not denounce De Sapio by name, nor did he even launch the kind of attack on the boss system that could be resented by the two other important boss figures, Buckley of the Bronx and Sharkey of Brooklyn. Instead, he took the position that De Sapio should "step aside" in the interest of party unity. He contended that De Sapio, by announcing his intended purge of the reformers, was creating party disharmony; that De Sapio should have been willing to listen to criticism and continue to work for a broad party base "constantly responsive to the needs of the community."

In a reply that was devoid of any of Baron's heated adjectives, De Sapio tried to point up the Mayor's dilemma:

I am sorry that Mayor Wagner has permitted himself to be euchered into his present position. I am sorry both for his sake and for the sake of the Democratic Party. In choosing sides—and in allying himself with a small group of people who seek to rule or ruin the Democratic Party—he has forsaken his friends, his supporters and his own conscience.

Mayors and political leaders come and go. What remains is the integrity and progress they represent and the impressions and records they leave behind. My responsibilities to the enrolled Democrats, both as New York County Chairman and National Committeeman, are such that I cannot allow myself to engage in a running fray with the Mayor at this moment. I think it best not to go into those questions and circumstances; those motives and influences which led to Mr. Wagner's unfortunate captivity.

Neither the Mayor nor I determine the party leadership or the party's candidates. The people will make that decision for themselves—as only they can—in the primary election.

De Sapio's reference to the people picking the party candidates in the primary was a thinly veiled threat to oppose the mayor if he sought nomination for a third term. In this he was premature. The mayor at that time was not at all sure he would run. He was increasingly concerned about the little time with his family that his duties as mayor permitted, and he was also worried about surgery that he himself faced. He deferred his final decision until June, but in his typically careful way, he also laid the groundwork for running if he chose.

In this period Wagner had tentative arrangements with Rose for getting the Liberal Party nomination. He had also encouraged his close ally, Harry Van Arsdale, the real boss of organized union labor in the city, to form a Brotherhood Party. This was a vehicle on which Wagner could run as an independent if he lost the Democratic nomination, although that purpose was never disclosed. And the mayor continued to court Buckley and Sharkey while attacking De Sapio, in case he did decide to enter the Democratic primary.

In June, to pave the way for the mayor's final, affirmative decision, a version of his plans was leaked, by Alex Rose as the mayor's agent, to *The New York Times*. The paper reported "on high authority" that Wagner had decided to run again, with a ticket of his own choosing that had Paul Screvane, his deputy mayor, as the nominee for president of the City Council, and Abe Beame, his budget director, as the nominee for controller.

The same "high authority" disclosed that if Abe Stark, the incumbent Council president, was interested, he could stay on the ticket as the nominee for controller, in which case Beame would run for borough president of Brooklyn. The story did not specify whether

175

the mayor planned to run in the Democratic primary, or as an independent on the Liberal and Brotherhood lines, or go after all three nominations.

The vagueness on the status of Stark and on the party nominations the mayor would seek was deliberate. It reflected two Wagner aims. One was to remove Stark from the line of succession to the mayoralty, which, as previously noted, Wagner felt militated against his own possible candidacy for higher office in the coming four years. The second aim was not to affront Sharkey, the Brooklyn boss. In a Democratic primary fight, the mayor would want the support of both Sharkey and Buckley, if possible.

In keeping with this, the Mayor summoned the two bosses to meet with him at Gracie Mansion the morning of the day he was to make his formal announcement of candidacy at City Hall, for which the press, the radio, and the TV networks had been alerted. De Sapio had met with his two colleagues on the previous day, and in that earlier session the trio reviewed the mayor's maneuvers and reflected on where it left them.

De Sapio, still the man the others looked to for advice, knew the spot they felt themselves to be on. His tack was to point out to them that support of a Wagner committed to reform would prove only a temporary painkiller. He said, in effect, "If Wagner is reelected, I'm in the ashcan. That's all right, that's politics. But he'll be pushed further and further by this reform crowd, and do you know who will get the gate next? First you, Joe," pointing his finger at Sharkey, "and then you, Charley, whether you support him now or not."

Buckley and Sharkey were impressed with the logic, but not completely convinced. They decided on a test which would show whether De Sapio was right or whether they could really count on the mayor. At Gracie Mansion they told Wagner they were willing to support him for renomination provided they were allowed to name the balance of the ticket, which would give them patronage protection as well as Board of Estimate influence. Buckley even brought to the conference, for the mayor's inspection, Buckley's selection for controller, an obscure Bronx judge of Italian descent.

Wagner first ruled the possible controller out of the conference

—had him wait on the Gracie Mansion porch—and then ruled him out of consideration entirely. Buckley turned to the mayor and said, "All right, Bob, you pick an Italian from the Bronx. Pick anyone you want." Wagner replied, "Charley, I don't know too many of your Bronx Italians and I don't see how I can run with someone I don't know."

Sharkey, for his part, declined to commit himself to the dumping of Stark, though he did not rule it out completely. Instead, the two bosses pressed for an arrangement whereby Wagner would limit his own announcement that day to the mayoralty, with the balance of the ticket to be picked later. Buckley appealed to the author, who was present, for support of this gambit.

"Why can't he just announce his own candidacy today?" Buckley insisted.

"I could tell you, Charley, but you'd get mad."

"Tell me anyhow."

"All right, you asked for it. It adds up to this. If the mayor announces his own candidacy and holds up the rest of his ticket, it will look to the public as if he were waiting to hear from the bosses. And the bosses aren't the most popular people in town."

After this interchange Wagner and his aides left for City Hall, and Buckley and Sharkey remained at Gracie Mansion to await a telephone call that would give them Wagner's final answer. In the mayor's car on the way downtown it was agreed finally that Wagner, at this stage of the game, had no alternative but to proceed with his original program, even if it involved the alienation of Buckley and Sharkey. At City Hall he went into his televised press conference to announce his bid for a third term and his independent selection of Screvane and Beame as his running mates. Buckley and Sharkey, having gotten the phone call from City Hall, went by taxicab to the Hotel Biltmore, where De Sapio awaited them.

The three bosses, shortly joined by their counterparts from Queens and Richmond—both De Sapio allies—proceeded over the next few days to whip up their own ticket. For mayor they picked Arthur Levitt, the state controller, with an up-to-then impeccable record both as a vote getter and an officeholder. Levitt, from Brooklyn, was Jewish. For ethnic and geographic balance, his running mates were Tom Mackell, a Queens Irishman, for president of the City Council, and Joseph De Fede, a Manhattan Italian, for controller. Stark was placated by being put up for borough president of Brooklyn, with nomination and election guaranteed, since the Wagner forces did not oppose him.

It was all carefully worked out to present the maximum in strength, but the bosses might have saved themselves the trouble. In the name-calling campaign that followed—the bitterest in the city's political history—the candidates on the boss-picked slate, even Levitt, were virtually ignored. In the three months between the June nominations and the September primary, the public heard only of the demerits of Wagner from one side and of the wickedness of De Sapio, Buckley, Sharkey, et al., from the other.

Wagner's second term in office had been good, but not up to his first. In the last year of his second term there was a scandal involving the rigging of school construction bids by the hierarchy of the Board of Education, and the education system itself was beginning to show the deterioration that would accelerate into rapid decline. While the Board of Education was independent of the mayor, he had appointed its members and bore the responsibility for its deficiencies. In addition, crime in the streets was beginning to worry the populace. And the city-aided construction of needed new housing was lagging. After much turmoil within and without the city administration a new agency was just beginning to struggle with the problem.

In the face of these liabilities Wagner, after conferences with Rose and the pollster Louis Harris, decided to run in the Democratic primary, as well as on the Liberal and Brotherhood tickets, as the candidate who stood against the bosses. Harris's polls, taken privately for Wagner, showed that "bossism" was the only issue on which he could win. The mayor, ever the pragmatist, adopted it not only against De Sapio but against the entire quintet of county leaders who opposed him, even Buckley, whom he had courted so long.

The bosses in turn became irate, losing their political judgment and perspective, and ran exactly the kind of campaign against Wagner that was his major guarantee of success. Instead of sticking to the back room and letting Levitt make the race, they took on themselves the onus of answering the mayor and attacking him, thus publicly exposing themselves each day as men who acted as if they had the most at stake.

De Sapio himself was the worst offender against political common sense. He acted as the ringmaster of the Levitt campaign, and the anti-boss press delighted in reporting the occasions when Levitt had not even been apprised of the content of some statement issued in his name, which had been handed to the press by Sydney Baron after De Sapio had approved it.

De Sapio in his own name charged Wagner with having permitted someone doing business with the city to pay Wagner's hotel bill at the 1960 national convention, which, he averred, made Wagner "legally, morally and politically ineligible for any public office, least of all mayor." In another blast he ridiculed Wagner for having "had eight years of doing nothing and now he wants to clean up in City Hall the mess he took eight years to make."

Mike Prendergast, De Sapio's echo, lent his name to a Baron-inspired statement that "Wagner sold out his moral obligations for alliances with the spoilers of hypocrisy." On his own, speaking in his capacity as state chairman, Prendergast declared that "a Wagner win will mean the destruction of the Democratic Party."

Sharkey, replying to a Wagner charge that the bosses had been stumbling blocks in the path of progressive legislation, called the mayor a "bare-faced liar." He recalled that the Mayor had publicly wrapped his arms around Sharkey and praised him, in his role as majority leader of the City Council, for pushing through liberal legislation against tremendous obstacles. Sharkey added that "those who have watched the Wagner career are not unused to seeing men who served him left in his path with knives in their backs."

Wagner ignored Levitt and hammered away daily on his one issue. He declared that "De Sapio marked 1961 as the year he and his gang were going to take over City Hall and the Board of Estimate."

"The boss system," said the Mayor, "has a demoralizing effect. Ending it will lead to greater safety on the streets, better housing and better schooling. The bosses are not interested in what is taught in the schools, but who gets the construction contract and who gets the architects' fees."

Julius Edelstein, released by Lehman to write Wagner's speeches, contributed some unconscious humor by hitting at his opposite number in the De Sapio camp, Sydney Baron. He put into Wagner's mouth these words: "The boss system under De Sapio has been merchandized by the constant services of a public relations expert. So integral a part of De Sapio's operation has this become that a lucrative public relations business has been built on boss influence peddling. It is a new form of invisible government."

Since the alleged influence peddling had been largely within the Wagner administration itself, the logic of making De Sapio responsible for Wagner's permissiveness was somewhat strained. But logic played a minor role in the campaign, as witness the characterization by Ed Cavanagh, Wagner's campaign manager, of the opposition as led by "demons and depraved maniacs." A charge issued in Levitt's name that the Wagner forces were guilty of anti-Semitism was in the same category.

The name calling in the mayoralty contest was only part of the action in the primary. De Sapio, implementing his February threat of a purge of the reform leaders, entered candidates for district leader and county committeemen in each of the reform districts; the reformers in turn invaded De Sapio territory. While not all the slates survived the intricate election-law requirements for petition gathering and filing, there were valid contests in parts of each of Manhattan's sixteen assembly districts, a real county-wide fight for control.

Both sides recognized that the key battle was in Greenwich Village, where for the third time the reformers sought to topple the De Sapio pyramid of power by gaining control of the base. The top reform leadership, after canvassing a broad field for a strong candidate to carry the anti-De Sapio banner in his home territory, found their man in James E. Lanigan, a Harvard Law School graduate, who had developed a taste for politics in his native Nebraska. The forty-three-year-old Lanigan was a Stevenson man, well known as such. He had started his government career in Washington as an aide to Averell Harriman when the latter was Mutual Security Administrator. Then Harriman lent him to the Stevenson camp for both the 1952 and 1956 presidential campaigns, in which he handled the scheduling of Stevenson's appearances in the eastern third of the United States. Between Washington assignments and presidential campaigns, Lanigan had become a New Yorker and was a founder of a reform club in the Gramercy Park area, close by the Village.

The trio who took on the task of drafting Lanigan to make the race were no less than Adlai Stevenson himself, Herbert Lehman, and Eleanor Roosevelt. They summoned Lanigan to a luncheon conference and offered support if he would run. When he showed himself less than eager, they insisted it was his obligation to do so, to them personally as well as to the reform movement. They recalled past favors and the image of more to come.

They promised to knock heads together among the cantankerous Village Independent Democrats to ensure reform unity, which had been lacking there in the past; Lehman personally guaranteed raising the $50,000 that had been budgeted for the Greenwich Village fight. They eventually carried through on both promises. Lanigan was accepted without too much dissent at a VID mass meeting, and Robert M. Benjamin and Lloyd K. Garrison, long-time fund raisers for the Stevenson wing of the party, raised most of the money at a Harvard Club luncheon. Lehman made up the balance.

Once Lanigan agreed to run, he plunged with vigor and enthusiasm into the fray. He sold his cooperative apartment on Gramercy Park and moved into a rented one on Washington Square. He personally canvassed the Village house by house to get out the vote of any Democrats previously uncommitted or uninterested. Years later he admitted he had even smoked pot with the early generation of beatniks, then staging the first invasion of the Village. De Sapio realized the serious threat the Lanigan candidacy contained, and he counter-campaigned as he had not bothered to do against his two earlier opponents.

Even though the Village was the home of the boss, it was one area of the city where the boss issue figured less importantly than others. The Village had its own problems, about which it voiced its concern through loud and articulate spokesmen. There was the threat of a widened roadway through Washington Square Park, a Robert Moses dream designed to create a lower Fifth Avenue in Little Italy linked with the stately Fifth Avenue to the north; there were tenants facing eviction from old buildings to be razed for a spate of new apartment-house construction; there was overcrowding in the area's public schools; there was a rise in drug use and in the number of burglaries, committed by addicts in need of daily cash.

De Sapio ran at least even with Lanigan in handling the issues. Through his greater familiarity with city agencies and the men who ran them, he did produce results here and there for which he could properly claim the credit. The factors with which he could not cope were the changed Greenwich Village population, the enlarged boundaries of the district, and the mass anti-boss hysteria.

At the start of his career the neighborhood had been populated mostly by people who had been born in the Village and expected to die there. By 1961 it also housed a much more transient population. The district captains of the Tamawa Club could not even keep track of the new voters, find them in their homes, much less present an election-day claim in return for services rendered during the year. Legislative reapportionment had added to the district many more of the upper-crust residences of lower Fifth Avenue and the adjacent side-streets. The new arrivals were wealthier and therefore less dependent on traditional political services, and more issue-minded.

The Stevenson campaigns of 1952 and 1956 had added a new dimension to political campaigning. Instead of the headquarters arranging a rally which prospective voters might attend, but would probably ignore, some committed couple would arrange for a more intimate gathering in their own apartment, with friends and neighbors invited in for coffee or cocktails and a chance to meet the candidate. The technique had proven its effectiveness, and De Sapio perforce adopted it when he found that Lanigan was playing this cocktail-party circuit.

At one such party De Sapio, entering the living room to which he had been invited, spotted among the guests a girl who had always been one of his faithful adherents, and who was employed on her own merits in City Hall as an administrative assistant to one of Mayor Wagner's principal aides. He slipped quickly and unobtrusively to her side and asked, "Lil, are you all right?" meaning was she endangering her job. "Sure I am, Boss," she replied. "I'm civil service, with tenure."

He thought for a second and said, "Well, make sure you don't stick your neck out." Up to then he had had a supporter. From then on he had an idolator.

The primary, when it finally rolled around, proved all of De Sapio's home-district campaigning to have been in vain, and the five Democratic county machines to have been paper tigers.

The middle-class Jewish voters of the West Side and Washington Heights, Flatbush and Forest Hills, always Democratic, turned out in droves to manifest their independence of the traditional machines; the black areas of Harlem, Bedford-Stuyvesant, and South Jamaica, where formerly the vote could have been totaled accurately for the machine before it was even cast, showed a newborn independence. The Puerto Rican areas cast the heaviest pro-Wagner vote of all. Wagner had identified himself early in his career with this particular voting bloc. As mayor, Wagner had continued to give them political recognition. In the 1961 primary the bread thus cast came floating back. Many of the Puerto Rican areas went twenty to one for Wagner, and the vote was a heavy one.

All over the city De Sapio, his allied bosses, and the Levitt ticket were blasted by a record turnout for a primary election. The total vote was 742,810, of which 451,188 went to Wagner and 291,672 to Levitt. Screvane and Beame rode in on the Wagner tide, and so did many of the candidates for City Council, district leader, and county committee membership who ran on the pro-Wagner, anti-boss slate.

The anti-boss vote either toppled or discredited the existing county leadership in every county save the Bronx, where the benevolent ties of the old Flynn machine were still binding enough to preserve Buckley. In Manhattan the reformers won fourteen of the sixteen district contests, raising their actual membership on the Tammany executive committee to 28 out of 66, and increasing the vote they could cast from 3⅚ to 6⅚, of the total of 16 votes. The remaining 9⅙ votes were shared by the still independent black bloc and the loyal De Sapio supporters. The latter remained the largest voting bloc, but lacked the clear majority they had had from the day De Sapio had taken over the leadership twelve years before.

In the Village the vote for district leader was 6,165 for Lanigan and 4,245 for De Sapio. In his home election district the boss lost out for election to the humble seat of county committeeman by a vote of 100 to 84. When the polls closed and the ballots were counted that night, Carmine De Sapio was just one of the 2,202,162 enrolled Democrats in the city, registered, ironically enough, under the permanent personal registration system which had been one of his electoral reforms.

The political power that had been his never again was concentrated in one person. His county chairmanship automatically was vacated with the election of a new executive committee, and it took six months of behind-the-scenes negotiation for Bob Wagner to come up with De Sapio's successor, Edward Costikyan. Wagner refused to throw votes he controlled to the organized reform movement and finally persuaded the party regulars, black and white, to get behind Costikyan, who was a reform veteran on the committee, but not the choice of the reform movement to run the show. In the course of Costikyan's brief tenure the ancient name of Tammany Hall disappeared down the drain, and the organization was known thereafter under its legal name, the New York County Democratic Committee.

To the extent that the mayor exercised the city leadership, he did so through Alex Rose, presenting the anomaly of the Liberal Party leader handling Democratic patronage and problems. Mike Prendergast, the state chairman, had opposed Wagner in the primary, and the mayor happily handed his political head to the Prendergast enemies in the Kennedy administration. The Prendergast successor was William H. McKeen, an upstate Democrat with no great influence besides what the mayor chose to lend him at any moment. De Sapio's national committee membership, which he retained in name until 1964, was eventually filled by Edwin L. Weisl, a New York lawyer selected by Wagner because of Weisl's close relationship with the incumbent President, Lyndon Johnson.

The epilogue of the De Sapio political career dragged on four years after the 1961 defeat, through three successive primary fights studded with recounts and court actions reminiscent of the days of his uphill battle against the Finn dynasty.

When he lost the last time, in 1961, he described himself the day after the primary as "a lively corpse, down but not out." And he meant it. He couldn't conceive of permanent victory for the forces that had conquered him. He looked at the reform movement and accurately predicted that there was too much disorder and lack of discipline in the reform ranks for it to survive as an effective machine. He was sure he could stage a comeback. He was encouraged when Lanigan, his Village successor, found it too wearing to try to get along amicably with the discordant VID and did not run for reelection in 1963. He drew more comfort from the fact that his able assemblyman, William F. Passanante, survived the De Sapio tag he bore and was reelected in 1962, with the blessings of both Mayor Wagner and Senator Lehman.

When De Sapio ran for district leader again in 1963 it was against a new opponent, one of the original organizers of the VID, Edward R. Koch. It was a fairly lively campaign. Koch at one point raised the issue of whether De Sapio favored integration, and De Sapio's retort was that it was akin to asking him where he stood on motherhood. De Sapio this time came very close to winning.

As the closing hour for the polls neared, the Koch group woke up to the fact that the vote had been light in the VID strongholds and that Little Italy was voting as ever, and just as strong in numbers, for De Sapio. Koch and his friends rushed from apartment to apartment, getting out supporters who had not bothered to vote. A few reached the polls in their night clothes. The tally on the voting machines was 4,656 for Koch and 4,615 for De Sapio, a margin of just 41 votes.

Just as he had done decades before against Finn, De Sapio took his case to the courts. He proved that there were fifteen more votes on the machines than there were names signed on the registry books;

he proved also that twenty members of the Liberal Party, all presumably anti-De Sapio, had been improperly permitted to vote in the Democratic primary. But the State Supreme Court justice who heard the case held that the irregularities proven were insufficient to have been deciding, and Koch took his seat as the victor.

The contest had been all but forgotten when on May 7, 1964, the state's highest court, the Court of Appeals, ruled that a new primary election should be held. A primary for public and party offices other than district leadership was already on tap for June 2, and the Village leadership was added to the list.

There was time for only a quickie campaign, waged by sound trucks and canvassing on the never-quiet Village streets. De Sapio toured with his elderly father, Gerard, and his attractive daughter, injecting a family note he had hitherto avoided. This time, though the total vote was larger, so was Koch's margin of victory, 5,904 to 5,470. De Sapio mustered up the fortitude for one more try—the primary of the mayoralty year 1965—when the trend was again anti-machine, and again he lost, 5,895 to 5,282.

In all of these efforts De Sapio contended that he was seeking only the post of Democratic leader of the Village, that he had no eye on any larger area of operations. Since he never regained his executive committee seat, he never was tempted. That he retained substantial influence within the executive committee of the New York County Democratic Committee—née Tammany Hall—could not be doubted.

By the spring of 1964 Ed Costikyan felt he could no longer stand being the man in the middle, without real power, in the constant friction between Mayor Wagner and the faction-torn executive committee. He resigned abruptly. Then came J. Raymond Jones, the first black man to head Tammany. Jones, who was anything but a reformer, kept tenuous control for a time, until his ulcers got the better of him and he resigned for reasons of health. His successor was Frank Rossetti, De Sapio's close confidant during the days of glory, the man who had chauffeured him around in his car, acting as bodyguard as well as friend, and who had remained loyal to him in all the troubled years.

THE FINANCES OF A BOSS

A ll the years that Carmine De Sapio was a political leader, and even later as a still prominent and influential citizen, he and his wife and daughter lived comfortably but not ostentatiously. The rewards of success showed themselves principally in more expensive housing. The De Sapios moved successively from their six-room, $55-a-month Charlton Street apartment to much higher priced quarters on Washington Square—in a building in which Eleanor Roosevelt for a time had her pied-à-terre—and then to an even newer and more fashionable apartment house at 11 Fifth Avenue. Even so, the apartment was small, and the De Sapios owned no summer home in exurbia or winter hideaway in the Caribbean.

Mrs. De Sapio and their daughter dressed well and had ample pocket money, but they were not among those who showed up daily at the smartest shops or fashionable restaurants. De Sapio himself had no particular affection for big-time gambling or betting on the races, he drank only modestly, and he was too tied up in politics for extended, expensive vacations abroad or even in this country. He did frequent good restaurants and never hesitated in reaching for the check. All in all, the family lived on a scale which appeared to reflect a 1950s income of $35,000 or $40,000 a year.

If this was anywhere near an indication of total income, it was a modest return for so high-ranking a political boss. Tom Pendergast of Kansas City gambled away millions at the racetrack, until even a reluctant Internal Revenue Service, which rarely initiated action against political bosses, had to take notice. Frank Hague of Jersey

City maintained expensive apartments and staffs in New York and Florida, and was constantly fighting off investigating committees seeking to know what he had stowed away in various safe-deposit boxes. The list of high-living bosses could go on indefinitely.

The De Sapio scale of living nevertheless was beyond what the family breadwinner earned in his highest-salaried post connected with public affairs—$20,000 a year as secretary of state of the State of New York—and it was assumed, by those who thought of it at all, that he did have outside income. What was its source?

The citizen has a schizoid attitude on the subject of the income of political leaders. As a party member he expects full-time service, but as a taxpayer he rejects the idea that politicians should be paid a public salary for what they do as party officials, and he is less than friendly to the idea of their holding some public office and getting paid for doing no public work; he really shows no interest in how they do make a living until confronted with evidence that they have done so illegitimately, and then he settles back comfortably reassured of his own sagacity in believing that all politicians are grafters. The citizen is reinforced in this belief by his own knowledge of how many upright citizens like himself have offered bribes to buy special privileges and have had their offers accepted.

The public prosecutor is always happy to give immunity to the citizen who paid the bribe, to get at the politician who accepted it. He justifies this on the grounds that public office is a public trust, and besides, he would get no convictions at all any other way. This type of thinking has even spilled over into the jury room, as witness the justice dealt out in one of the great scandals of American government, Teapot Dome. Albert B. Fall, Secretary of the Interior, was convicted and jailed for accepting a bribe from oil magnate Harry F. Sinclair. Sinclair, at a separate trial, was acquitted of having given that same bribe to Fall.

In New York City the cruder types of graft, such as dipping directly into the public till by means of false invoices or payroll padding, have been obsolete for years as far as the top political leadership is concerned. Neither has anyone attempted in modern times to enjoy a percentage "off the top" of public contracts, from which

Hague and Pendergast in particular made so many millions. In Murphy's time there grew up the concept of "honest graft." This sometimes involved buying up land on the basis of inside knowledge that it would be needed for a pending public improvement; it went as far as holding up permits for construction by private industry until the contract was awarded to a politically favored firm. Even this form of larceny was discarded at public demand. In recent times, with rare exceptions, the illegitimate profit on contracts with the city government has been garnered by rings of contractors who buy up minor city officials without the connivance of the top political leadership.

As a result the political elite, in order to make anything from a comfortable living to a sizable fortune, go in for businesses which by their nature offer a front for the selling or lending of political influence. For a long time the most popular fronts were law firms and insurance companies. They have been joined in recent years by architecture and public relations firms. All have in common the fact that their services cannot be arranged for by competitive public bidding, their fees can be based on what the traffic will bear, and there can be no probative evidence of why one firm was selected in preference to another.

In one era, various people in the New York Republican Party accumulated substantial fortunes practicing as the attorneys for liquor-license seekers before the Republican-controlled state liquor-licensing board. The size of the legal fees bore no relation to the amount of paper work involved, time consumed, or legal talent required, but directly reflected the success of the properly connected lawyer in winning the board's favor.

One leader of Tammany Hall in the late 1920s made more than $3 million in fees in just five years of practice before a particular city agency. The agency—the Board of Standards and Appeals—had the power to grant builders of office structures and large apartment houses a relaxation of the zoning laws on hardship grounds. The board judged the hardship. Applicants were willing to pay tremendous fees to any lawyer, such as the leader of Tammany Hall, who could guarantee the board's indulgence.

Another De Sapio predecessor as leader of Tammany Hall used his political power to build a small insurance agency into a very large and prosperous one. He controlled the man who ran the Manhattan Department of Buildings, which inspected all properties to make sure they complied with the building code. Those who did business with the boss's insurance agency received no notice of violations; those who refused to switch to his agency from their original brokers found every minute provision and technicality of the law used against them.

A long-time Democratic leader in Queens and successive leaders in Brooklyn prospered through an offshoot of the insurance business, the furnishing of performance bonds for contractors doing public work. The political help they could give the contractors got them the bonding business.

There have also been influential law firms, with congressmen and senators prominent among the "name" partners, which sold their influence without really practicing law for their clients. They accepted fees for simply putting their names as "of counsel" on briefs filed with a court or regulatory agency. An exception to this was the law firm headed by Ed Flynn. He and his principal partner, Monroe Goldwater, agreed at the outset—in 1922—that they were destined to be a "political" law firm, but laid down the rule that they would never sell the firm's name for an "of counsel" fee. They would insist on doing the actual legal work involved. The Goldwater & Flynn fees then reflected both the prominence of the Flynn name and the very considerable legal talents the firm offered.

Carmine De Sapio chose insurance as the business that would account for his outside income. During the 1940s and most of the 1950s he maintained a small agency in the insurance district on John Street, under the name of Carmine G. De Sapio & Co. Starting in 1959, when he left state office on the heels of Harriman's defeat for reelection as governor, he became a vice-president of the Jay B. Rappaport Company, at a published salary of $25,000 a year.

Rappaport was a prosperous general insurance agency with midtown offices not far from the center of political activity at the Hotel

Biltmore. De Sapio could be found at one set of offices or the other and had secretaries at both. Actually, De Sapio never worked at the insurance business, for Rappaport or anyone else. He was not a licensed broker, and did not act as though he was. It was assumed that to the Rappaport Company he was worth his salary for his contacts, as a business getter. Just his identification with the firm would bring in customers who thought it worthwhile to do a favor for the boss, in case they wanted a favor themselves sometime.

During the years De Sapio kept his own little John Street insurance office, he did not even seek clients for it. He accepted the business of some who came his way, which he passed on to partners, provided the account did not present a conflict of loyalties, of which he was very conscious.

In the light of the charges against him later when he was a private citizen—and his trial and conviction on them—two incidents are revealing of the care De Sapio took in protecting his position against criticism while he was the principal political agent of the mayor.

In the late 1950s the relationship between the Wagner city administration and the governmental empire built by Robert Moses around the Triborough Bridge and Tunnel Authority was beginning to be strained. Moses's failures in one of his satellite operations, the Slum Clearance Committee, were weakening Wagner's confidence in the veteran master builder. No overt break had yet occurred, but Moses could sense difficulties. He sent for De Sapio and offered him the insurance contracts for the billion-dollar Triborough properties. De Sapio graciously declined, explaining that he did not think his firm was big enough to handle it. He confided later to the author that he felt he was being offered the very substantial commissions involved because of influence he had with the mayor and that for him to accept Moses's favor would have implied his own commitment to be in Moses's corner.

On the other hand, he did accept, and referred to a political associate for handling, a similar insurance account for the New York City Housing Authority. The operating head of that agency sought out De Sapio to make the offer to avoid pressures he was getting from other insurance agencies, with good political connections, for the Housing Authority business. In this case De Sapio saw no conflict of interest.

His recognition of a genuine conflict-of-interest situation was unusual, almost unique, because such situations are seldom encountered, are almost nonexistent. The term "conflict of interest" has grown in use because it has come to be applied to either:

1. A genuinely innocent situation—such as inconsequential stock ownership in a corporation that starts doing business with government—in which the government official or political leader could benefit, even though there was no original connection between the stock interest and the awarding of the contract. This presents the appearance of conflict of interest without the reality.

2. A straight cover-up for graft or influence selling, with the politician receiving by arrangement either fees or stock ownership in return for influencing favorable governmental action. As such, it is a device designed to furnish reasonable doubt which might keep a jury from sending the participants to jail.

De Sapio avoided anything which could be interpreted as using his influence for personal gain as long as he acted as agent for others. Yet he lived comfortably and obviously had outside income, other than that derived from the insurance business, which insiders in politics identified as flowing from several sources.

First was his relationship with Sydney Baron. Baron came into De Sapio's life in the 1953 mayoralty primary campaign, De Sapio's first major stride toward success. The bubbling press agent became a social as well as business associate of the boss, was with him many hours of the day, wrote many of his statements and speeches, and contributed these services, it was assumed, without fee. Baron prospered as a result of the relationship far beyond any cash fee De Sapio could have paid.

Baron set himself up in traditional Madison Avenue press-agent surroundings, with plush offices and lush receptionists and secretaries. He spread the word that he was the intimate of the boss and waited for the customers to roll in. They did, in short order. There were a large number of big-business clients, including some of America's great corporate names, to whom it seemed advantageous to have on the payroll a PR man with such obvious entree into politics and government. This had always been a commonplace for them in their dealings with Congress and the executive branch of government in Washington, but it was brand-new in New York City. No PR man prior to Baron had connections so well recognized and firmly established. It was generally assumed that De Sapio received a share of some of Baron's fees, simply because the relationship otherwise made little sense.

As De Sapio's close associate, Baron could furnish quick and easy entree for his clients to City Hall and the state capitol in Albany. Commissioners, state department heads, staff aides of the mayor and the governor readily answered his telephone calls and gave his clients the red-carpet welcome. The clients were impressed, and Baron's fees were substantial—and earned—even when nothing more in the way of special favor could be granted. This happened quite often.

In the Wagner administration in particular there was an unspoken rule against the granting of any favor that if published could reflect on the good name of the administration. This stemmed from the mayor himself. He was jealous of the good name of Wagner, and he was independently wealthy enough to scorn opportunities to make more money. He expected his aides to reject any favoritism sought by the politically-connected where money was involved. This sometimes worked against the mayor himself. There were several occasions on which he was sold a bill of goods by some particularly adroit favor-seeker and turned the request over to an aide, with his endorsement, for implementation. His aide would check the facts and reject the course the mayor had consented to. On at least one occasion, the mayor suspected an aide was prejudiced and had the rejection checked by another. When both reports jibed, the mayor dropped the matter.

This type of checking affected Baron the same as it did anyone else. Although given preferential treatment in the form of quick access and the cutting of red tape, he never got a favor for a client that broke the standing rules. What was more remarkable was the fact that there never was any follow-up pressure from De Sapio for additional consideration for his friend.

On one occasion a city commissioner, a friend of De Sapio's who had a special background in the labor field, was asked by De Sapio to check a speech being written for him by Baron which involved labor policies. The commissioner called Baron, who asked as a favor that the commissioner meet him in Baron's uptown office. A date was set, and when the commissioner arrived to discuss the speech he found Baron with a client who did business with the commissioner's own agency. Baron said it was a coincidence, but the commissioner stalked out indignantly. He felt it was a Baron stunt to impress the client.

If Carmine De Sapio had a financial interest in Sydney Baron's activities, the policy of noninvolvement on the part of the boss again reflected unusual discretion. Influence peddling in the guise of public relations service was a common practice among far less influential politicians, particularly state legislators and members of both houses of Congress.

A second source of income open to the boss stemmed from the fact that so much political money passed from one hand to another in cash. Take the system De Sapio installed in connection with the selection and promotion of judges. A lawyer seeking a place on the bench had to be marked as qualified by his local bar association, but if he had a substantial record of political service behind him, the party owed him recognition for it and he needed no more. But if he was not thus qualified politically, he needed cash.

The lawyer seeking his first place on the bench or the lower-court judge seeking promotion to a higher court made a cash "contribution" to the organization, for which there was no public accounting. Few men on the bench would even admit it privately, since they did not like to think, or have it thought about them, that they had bought their way in. They preferred to adopt the official explanation that they were contributing to organization campaign expenses. Political insiders believed that the money which came in that door was divided three ways—a share to the organization for expenses, a share for the district leader who had originally sponsored the applicant, and a share for the boss.

A "contributor" who paid by check for a bench nomination or any other consideration knew that his act and the amount he gave would eventually be publicized by inclusion in the statements of receipts and expenditures that the law requires of political groups and parties. And he might not want to be identified. He might have given to both sides in a primary or general election, to be sure of a friend at court no matter which side won; he might be so closely identified with a special interest that his contribution could be held up as a reason why the special interest should not benefit from a favor or be awarded a contract; he might have given cash because he thought the recipient would prefer it that way, so that he could personally pocket a portion of it. Whatever the reasoning, there have been more contributions made in cash, and for greater amounts, than ever show up in anyone's receipt records.

A third source of revenue open to De Sapio was the Moses empire. Moses, who was never vulnerable to the accusation of profiting financially from his widespread operations, nevertheless had no objections to others doing so, if they were useful to him.

Moses's principal aide became quite wealthy as a result of business opportunities that his official position opened up to him. He had as an associate in some of these a banker and Democratic Party fund raiser named Thomas J. Shanahan. And Shanahan was a close associate of De Sapio.

As the relationship between De Sapio and Wagner cooled, but before it was broken off completely, De Sapio was drawn into the Moses orbit through Shanahan's connections. As a result, Sydney Baron appeared as public relations counselor for a number of Title I housing projects, over which Moses had jurisdiction. Also, De Sapio was credited with an interest in the insurance agency for the 1964 New York World's Fair, of which Moses was the grand Pooh Bah.

Finally, there was Con Edison, the world's largest public utility company. De Sapio had close friends, like Michael J. Merkin, the paint manufacturer, who were on the Con Ed board of directors all the years De Sapio was the city's main political power. It was natural, even traditional, for big public utility companies to have friends among the men who controlled the city in which they were based. It began before the turn of the century as a two-way street—the district leader could always place a needy constituent in a job "down at the gas works," and the utility had no trouble getting the permits it needed to do work in the city streets. Protection of the utility against consumer groups demanding lower rates was, in New York at least, more the assignment of the Republican Party than of the Democrats, since large financial interests were involved in setting the rate structure. Con Edison, under various corporate names, had been a politically oriented organization throughout its history.

Anthony Brady, an Albany ex-bartender with a genius for finance, came down to New York City before the turn of the twentieth century with a plan for establishing a public utility monopoly. There were then half a dozen gas companies competing among themselves, but also facing extinction with the advent of electric light and power. The electric companies numbered at least a dozen, but they were relatively weak financially and definitely not making the most of Edison's great invention.

Brady persuaded the leading financiers of the day, Russell Sage, William Rockefeller, and J. Pierpont Morgan, that it would pay everybody to arrange a merger of the competing gas companies— which included Sage, Rockefeller, and Morgan interests—after which the new gas monopoly would take over the electric companies. The plan was carried out, and the Consolidated Gas Company emerged as the overall owner of both sources of power, though the names of the companies it absorbed stayed on the books for generations.

The Brady plan required permission of the state legislature, and little bills which nobody noticed slipped through in Brady's behalf. Brady bought and sold politicians at many levels during his money-making career. When he died in 1912 he left an estate of $200 million, although it was appraised for tax purposes at only $80 million by a friendly Albany Surrogate judge. His family owned a majority interest in the giant utility until 1929, when they sold out at the peak of the bull market. However, the company tradition, established by the Bradys, of having friends in high political office

196

continued uninterrupted from the original consolidation at the turn of the century into the late 1960s.

What has never been disclosed is that the money that was needed to maintain that friendship was spent by Consolidated from a private pocketbook, a subsidiary that had unlimited, unaudited funds.

The regular revenues and expenditures of a public utility are regulated by the Public Service Commission, which cannot approve money spent for political purposes, and federal as well as state statutes bar such use of corporate funds. However, back in 1885, at the very start of electric power distribution, it appeared as though the competing electric companies would constantly be tearing up city streets to put in their own conduits. To alleviate the problem the legislature granted a single company, the Consolidated Electric Telegraph and Subway Company, the right to lay electric conduits, with the obligation that it lease space in them to the competing companies. As a result of Brady's mergers the old Consolidated Gas Company became the majority stockholder in the "subway company"—as it was called—as early as 1898, and when it wiped out its other subsidiaries in 1936, the sole stockholder.

Consolidated continued to maintain the subway company as a separate entity, and by 1959 Con Edison—the new name for the old monopoly—was paying its wholly owned subsidiary $26 million a year rental for the underground conduits. The subway company was netting $7 million a year after taxes from the arrangement. It was not under the jurisdiction of the Public Service Commission, which had not come into existence until two decades after the subway company was formed by special statute. The sole requirement was that it file generalized reports—never audited—with the city Department of Water Supply, Gas and Electricity. Thus the subway company could accumulate a large surplus, which it did. It also could pay out what it pleased, to whom it pleased, with no supervision and no publicity. Con Edison's payments to politicians came from the subway-company coffers.

This very convenient arrangement might have gone on forever had not Con Edison in 1960 needed all the capital it could lay its hands on, for expansion purposes. It turned, as one source, to the subway company, which had accumulated more than $100 million in idle cash, and merged the old subsidiary into its main corporate structure. In so doing, it lost its private pocketbook.

The Con Edison managers—paid employees rather than owners with substantial blocks of stock in the company—arranged a substitute system for the flow of untraceable cash. It consisted of encouraging the rigging of bids by outside contractors competing for Con Edison's construction work. This in effect tapped the company till for monies which could be shared three ways—by the members of the contractors' ring, by leading politicians whose favor the company wanted to retain, and by the cooperating Con Edison executives.

Henry Fried, one of the principal contractors involved, was pictured later as having boasted that he had De Sapio and Vincent Albano, the New York County Republican leader, "in my pocket."

The system was in effect from 1960, when the subway company was merged into the main structure, to 1966, when Con Edison's bankers, disappointed in the company's financial progress, insisted on bringing in new top management, with Charles F. Luce as chairman and chief executive officer. Luce was not a New Yorker, was unaware of how political favor had been bought by the company in the past, knew nothing of the padded construction bids, and never considered adopting such practices as his own. His principal aides, all brought in from the outside, were equally innocent.

To the old ring of contractors, as well as their friends in politics and within the company, this represented incredible naiveté. They assumed the Luce group could be educated in the realities of corporate life in a big city. Their failure to realize that the old system was gone turned out to be disastrous for them: they were investigated, indicted, and exposed.

It was especially ironic that Carmine De Sapio—who had so carefully avoided using pressure for private profit when he was the city's top political power—was, as a private citizen, convicted of having conspired to extort money from a company which had only so recently been shoveling out its funds without any prodding at all.

THIRTEEN

THE END OF THE LINE

On December 13, 1969, Carmine De Sapio was convicted by a federal court jury of having conspired to induce a public official to misuse his office in return for a cash bribe.

At the time this happened De Sapio had been out of the political limelight for four years, the public official involved was already a thief with no assistance from De Sapio, and the politics De Sapio had known for most of his life no longer existed. The boss system of which he had been so outstanding a product was recalled, if at all, only contemptuously, and the charges against De Sapio linked him with a supposed "reform" city administration and a whole cast of disreputable characters with whom he had had no previous association.

If one assumes that the jury was correct in finding De Sapio guilty, there is an obvious cry for an explanation of why he as a private citizen would do the things he had refrained from doing when he was political boss and the opportunities were so much greater. As De Sapio himself said in District Attorney Hogan's office when he was first questioned about taking money and passing some of it along for the purpose of bribing a public official: "I wouldn't have done that thirty years ago, when I was an amateur."

One possible explanation, supportable completely by the record, is that De Sapio always abided by the rules of the game, whatever they were at the moment. When he first became a district leader and Tammany Hall was controlled by the underworld, he made no effort to change the system. When he became leader of Tammany Hall and Frank Costello suggested that he run a clean operation that would reflect credit on Italians in politics, he adopted that course eagerly and enthusiastically. When he worked with Wagner and Harriman, whose programs called for the avoidance of anything that was improper or even looked improper, De Sapio played ball. When he participated in the allocation of judgeships in return for cash, he was doing what had always been done, only much less crassly.

After this brand of politics was rejected by the voters—unjustly in De Sapio's mind—he moved in circles where money had always been passed under the table to secure some desired result: the business world of kickbacks and finders' fees, rebates, tax evasion, and bribery. He may easily have adopted the mores of private business once he was no longer under the obligation to maintain the higher degree of ethics and integrity demanded of those in public life.

The chain of events that preceded De Sapio's trial started with Bob Wagner's decision in 1965 not to seek a fourth term as mayor but to sit back and hope for a gubernatorial nomination—which he did not get—in 1966. Wagner opted to back Paul Screvane, the City Council president, for mayor, a selection which was contested in the Democratic primary by Abe Beame, the controller, William F. Ryan, the reformer, and I. D. Robbins, an independent. The winner was Beame, who had split earlier with Wagner on party politics and who by 1965 was the man closest to what was left of the Democratic machines in the five boroughs.

Alex Rose, still Wagner's political adviser and agent, would have given his Liberal Party blessing to Wagner for a fourth term, but in the light of the unpredictable Democratic primary contest, he had no sure Democratic nominee to endorse. Ever practical, Rose turned to John V. Lindsay, the attractive young Republican congressman who was assured of the Republican nomination. Rose had no trouble arranging a deal with Lindsay whereby if Lindsay won, the Liberal Party would receive half of the City Hall patronage. This "full partnership," as Rose used the science of semantics to describe it, was the most the Liberal Party had ever enjoyed.

The Liberal-Republican alliance would not have been enough to guarantee election, but other factors entered. One was the candidacy of William Buckley, the phrase-making idol of the political right, as the nominee of the newly important Conservative Party. Although the Conservatives were just as much an offshoot of the Republican Party as the Liberals were of the Democrats, Buckley drew more from the Democrats in the 1965 contest than he did from the Republicans. Conservative Democrats who had previously left their party for ideological reasons in contests for state and national office now defected for the first time in a mayoralty election.

Then there were the reformers. The old precept of majority rule had no meaning for them, and having lost in the primary, they swung to Lindsay in the election. Beame's organization-oriented candidacy lacked spark, and the wit, grace, and handsomeness of Lindsay, as well as his galaxy of promises, attracted Democratic "limousine liberals" and the upper middle classes generally. The combination of factors produced the first major crumbling of party lines, which previously had stood so firm at the municipal level.

Lindsay won by 102,000 votes, and while this was the smallest margin up to then for a mayoral winner, his election was hailed in the press as bringing city government back to the people and heralding a new era. Bob Wagner's wry comment was that "Lindsay was the best mayor the city ever had even before he took office."

Much of the ecstasy over Lindsay's victory stemmed from the candidate's own style and promises. People really believed he would bring the city something newer and fancier than Wagner, whose final four years had been humdrum. During the campaign, volunteers from all walks of life flocked into the Lindsay headquarters to see what they could do to help. One of these, willing to give his full time to the crusade without pay, was a darkly handsome jet-set type named James Marcus.

Marcus had no experience or background in politics. But he had a quick mind, a pleasing manner, plenty of energy, and a business background which he made sound much more substantial than it was. No one, then or later, bothered to check on his finances or his ethics in the face of his social credentials, which were impeccable. Marcus was married to the former Lilly Lodge, a close friend of Mary Lindsay, the candidate's wife. She was also the daughter of John Davis Lodge, a former governor of Connecticut and one of the

Lodges who dared speak to Lowells and Cabots in the family's original Boston habitat. Marcus moved surely and quickly from untried volunteer to membership in the inner circle of Lindsay activists.

After Lindsay took office as mayor on January 1, 1966, he pounded home his "new approach" to city government by ignoring the commissionerships and chains of command traditionally used to direct the day-by-day administration of the city's business. He had pledged the creation of ten superagencies which would do the job better than in the past, and while waiting for them to be born, he turned the operation of the departments over to a free-swinging group of young mayoral assistants. They bore no titles pertinent to any particular job but were armed with complete authority since they were direct emissaries of the mayor. Jim Marcus turned up as one of these, at the nominal salary of $1 per year. It was taken for granted, in the light of the society in which he moved, that he could afford to work for the glory alone.

One of Marcus's chief assignments was to run the Department of Water Supply, Gas and Electricity while the commissionership was deliberately left vacant to eliminate red tape. When Lindsay ran into insubordination on the part of another young assistant who was in charge of the Sanitation Department, Marcus was rushed in as troubleshooter to fill that spot as well. Early in the second year Marcus was sworn into the salaried job of water commissioner and was also designated to be the head of the Environmental Protection Administration—one of the superagencies—as soon as the City Council consented to its creation. Marcus seemed one of the most promising and effective of all of the young men around the new mayor.

No one knew that Marcus was not only broke but desperate. He had lost his own money and other people's in his shaky business enterprises. He had lost more in a stock-market plunge in an attempt to make a killing. He had landed in the hands of a big-time Mafia loan shark named Anthony "Tony Ducks" Corallo, who had already served a jail sentence for conspiracy to bribe a judge. To meet his debt to Corallo, Marcus was ready and willing to take bribes from contractors working for the Department of Water Supply.

Marcus could not have happened in a Tammany administration,

in which a man of loose morals might have been appointed, but not without full knowledge of his weaknesses. No one in the Lindsay administration looked behind the Marcus facade or checked into his bogus business references. It was just assumed that he was what he said he was.

But Marcus already was so committed to graft as his new way of life that he went directly from the City Hall ceremony at which he was promoted from a $1-a-year mayoral assistant to a full-fledged commissioner to a cocktail conference with Henry Fried, a contractor who was promising him cash for breaking his public trust.

The deal Marcus made with Fried was that he would award Fried's company an $800,000 contract to remove debris accumulated over the years in the Jerome Park Reservoir in the Bronx, through which most of the city water passed on its way from the watershed to the kitchen tap. In return Fried would kick back 5 percent—$40,000—part of which would go immediately to Corallo to help pay off Marcus's high-interest debt.

Marcus led his friend John Lindsay by the hand around the reservoir, for the benefit of reporters and photographers, to convince the public that the reservoir was a mess which the new administration was going to clean up swiftly. Marcus did this to create the impression that this was an emergency situation which would justify the awarding of the contract without public bidding.

It was the only way Fried could get the contract with certainty and Marcus the $40,000. The administration accepted the "emergency" concept, the work was done, the bribe was paid, and for months no one was the wiser except those who paid and got paid. Marcus was so encouraged by the success of this operation that he began paving the way for bigger and more profitable ones.

Then came trouble—which Marcus mistook for detection. Late in November 1967, District Attorney Hogan received a complaint from a lawyer in Philadelphia about one of Marcus's private business ventures. Hogan called in Marcus for his side of the story. Hogan found him evasive and shifty, and was convinced he was lying. There was a second, equally unsatisfactory interview. Hogan, notorious for his low boiling point, phoned Mayor Lindsay at City Hall and wanted to know what the hell kind of commissioners the city had.

It was the first Lindsay knew that Marcus had even been interviewed at Hogan's office. He called in Marcus, who explained that he did have some personal financial problems which did not involve the city, but he did think he should resign to devote full time to clearing them up. He and the mayor agreed on an exchange of letters. Marcus in his letter expressed regret at having to leave city service because of personal financial difficulties and professed his innocence of any "real wrongdoing."

Lindsay, either still completely trusting, or wishing to appear so, wrote back, "I do so [accept the resignation] with regret equal to yours because your performance in office has been excellent and our friendship, through governmental service and before, has been close. Mary [Mrs. Lindsay] joins me in sending best wishes to Lilly and yourself."

Hogan, continuing to press the ex-commissioner for a reasonable explanation of his private business dealings, became convinced that Marcus had become involved with loan sharks. He dropped the name of the leading one—Corallo—just to test Marcus's reaction. It was positive and immediate. Marcus left the DA's office and fled into the arms of a friend and companion in corruption, Herbert Itkin, who had originally involved him with Corallo and Henry Fried.

Itkin was a self-styled labor lawyer whose extracurricular activities became a continuing source of wonderment to state and federal prosecutors. Itkin had established himself years back as a paid informer for the Federal Bureau of Investigation while being involved in (and profiting from) a series of racketeering operations. The G-men would follow the leads Itkin had provided, investigate and turn over to federal prosecutors that which involved others in the racket, but would protect Itkin as a reward for his services as informer.

When Marcus told Itkin that Hogan was asking him about relations with Corallo, and therefore probably knew all about the reservoir contract and kickback, Itkin persuaded him that the best way to assure protection for both of them was for Itkin to lay the facts before his friends in the FBI. But while the FBI continued to protect Itkin, it did not extend its blanket to Marcus. It turned the facts over to the U.S. attorney for the Southern District of New York, Robert Morgenthau.

On December 18, 1967, six days after Mayor Lindsay so graciously accepted Marcus's resignation as Water Supply chief, Marcus and Corallo were arrested under federal indictments charging them with the reservoir kickbacks. Indicted with them were Henry Fried, a labor-union leader named Daniel Motto, and Charles Rappoport, Itkin's business partner.

Morgenthau had made a federal case of the scandal by acting under a law passed by Congress in 1961 as part of a federal anti-racketeering package drawn up by Attorney General Robert F. Kennedy. His indictments, sought without notifying Hogan, produced some rivalry and hard feelings between the offices of the two prosecutors. Hogan saw no reason why he should drop a case which had begun in his own office, and he continued to interrogate Marcus and the others identified in Morgenthau's indictments through Itkin's testimony.

Hogan was willing to give Itkin the same immunity from state prosecution in the reservoir case that the federal people had allowed, but no more, and he got no cooperation from Itkin as a result. But as he probed in other directions, he uncovered a real bombshell, the involvement of Carmine De Sapio.

How De Sapio's name reached Hogan's ears has never been disclosed before. One of Hogan's assistants was questioning Charles Rappoport, Itkin's law partner. Rappoport mentioned De Sapio as being involved in the operations of Marcus, Itkin, and Fried. Possibly Rappoport believed that bringing in the once powerful and still popular boss would ease the pressures on Rappoport and Itkin from Hogan's office. It had the opposite effect.

De Sapio and Hogan were friends. De Sapio had sponsored Hogan for U.S. senator, considered him for mayor, unhesitatingly renominated him every fourth year for district attorney. But in the prosecutor's office Hogan could not consider friendship. He was dedicated to an honest performance of the duties of the office, and so were the members of his staff; any soft-pedaling of a case would have ruined morale. When the staff reported Rappoport's hint, the very existence of Hogan's friendship with De Sapio compelled a thorough probe, with prosecution if warranted.

So Hogan beefed up the staff assigned to the loose ends of the Marcus case, putting five men to work full time on the assorted leads. He called in De Sapio, first on January 8, and again a week later for extended questioning by two of his assistants. On neither occasion was De Sapio subpoenaed, nor was there a stenographer in the room. De Sapio was offered the privilege of counsel, but he rejected it. It all seemed so informal. What De Sapio did not know was that the second interrogation was taped by a recorder in the next room, and his version of the story became part of the official record. Hogan, asked later by the author about what seemed to De Sapio and his friends a breach of courtesy, defended the practice as office routine, practiced in every case.

The things Hogan's assistants asked De Sapio about in no way involved the Jerome Park Reservoir contracts, but did include the same cast of characters—Marcus, Corallo, Fried, and Itkin.

As Itkin later testified, Corallo had suggested, after the reservoir deal had gone through so swimmingly, that Con Edison was a possible source of good income for Marcus and Itkin, if Marcus used his powers as water commissioner to the best advantage. Kickbacks could be got from contractors doing work for Con Edison if Con Edison could be persuaded to give those contractors the jobs, and Marcus, with full power over permits Con Edison constantly needed, had the leverage. Henry Fried thought so, too.

Fried had been a member of the ring of contractors who had been milking Con Edison for years through collusive bidding, and the ring had operated with the consent of some of Con Edison's top management officials. Fried was seeking new construction contracts from a new Con Edison management that had no idea of the practices that had previously existed. From Fried's point of view, Con Edison's top men had to be persuaded to play the game as it had always been played, and for this he needed a contact man.

Fried first tried Milton Lipkins, vice-president of the Broadway Maintenance Company, which through its contracts for street lighting had connections with both city and Con Edison officials, but Lipkins produced no results. Itkin testified that Fried later told him that the search for an effective intermediary had finally been successful. "I've got the man, Carmine De Sapio," Fried said, according to Itkin.

The Itkin version of the story amounted to this:

Fried, having decided on De Sapio as the intermediary between himself, Con Edison, and Commissioner Marcus, wanted to bring Itkin and De Sapio together to establish a relationship. Fried had already invited hundreds of friends and business associates to a lawn party at his horse farm at Germantown, New York, in the rolling hills of Columbia County, to be held August 20, 1967. That would be a good occasion for Itkin and De Sapio to meet, Fried thought.

He gave Itkin directions for getting to Columbia County—the county north of Dutchess on the east bank of the Hudson River—and this seemingly insignificant act became an important factor in the tragedy of Carmine De Sapio. According to Itkin, Fried said he could best avoid traffic by crossing the George Washington Bridge to New Jersey . . . and taking the Palisades Interstate Parkway to the New York State Thruway, then recrossing the Hudson on a bridge south of Germantown.

The normal route would have been to take the Saw Mill and Taconic parkways through Westchester, Putnam, and Dutchess counties to Germantown, never crossing the Hudson into New Jersey at all. A second choice would have been to take the Major Deegan Expressway out of New York City, hooking up with the Thruway in Westchester, crossing the Hudson on the Tappan Zee Bridge, and recrossing it seventy-five miles north, as in the route Itkin said he followed, again not entering New Jersey.

If there was a key point in the prosecution of Carmine De Sapio for conspiracy, it was in those driving directions that Itkin said Fried gave him, and which he said he followed. For this brought the "conspiracy" across a state line and thus within the jurisdiction of a federal court. Without the crossing into New Jersey, there was no federal case. And if there was no federal case, there probably was no case at all.

207

Under the 1961 Kennedy anti-racketeering statute, the testimony of the co-conspirators alone was sufficient to convict each and every one of them. Under long-standing New York State laws, there had to be corroboration from others who were not part of the conspiracy. Hogan never felt he had enough corroboration even to seek an indictment under the New York laws.

At De Sapio's trial in federal court, the defense counsel, Maurice Edelbaum, hit hard at Itkin's story that he had crossed the Hudson into New Jersey to get from one part of New York State to another, implying that the route had been concocted after the fact to justify the federal jurisdiction. But he had only his own note of disbelief to counteract Itkin's sworn testimony. Henry Fried, the man who gave the supposed directions, had won indefinite postponement of both questioning and trial on the certification of his doctors that his bad heart could not stand the strain.

The case against De Sapio had been developed without the fanfare that could have been expected in view of De Sapio's long-standing position in the political world. The first time the newspapers connected De Sapio with the Marcus scandal was during the Marcus trial, when they reported that De Sapio had been subpoenaed, and then excused from testifying after attorney Edelbaum conferred with the trial judge, Edward Weinfeld. Later in the Marcus trial Itkin referred to De Sapio's involvement while under cross-examination.

De Sapio, indicted on December 20, 1968, did not come to trial until November 12, 1969. The week before his case came up in the Federal Courthouse in Foley Square, John Lindsay had been re-elected mayor of New York after a campaign in which the remainder of the city's historic political structure collapsed completely. Lindsay, a Republican, lost his own party's nomination but was supported nevertheless by that party's hierarchy. Mario Procaccino emerged as a minority nominee from a multi-candidate Democratic primary but was deserted by almost every element of party leadership, as well as the rank and file. John Marchi, Republican-Conservative nominee, waged a quiet campaign which won him respect but not votes.

The majority of the Lindsay votes came from Democratic liberals and the black and Puerto Rican communities, which up to that election had been solidly Democratic. It was a topsy-turvy election of the kind Carmine De Sapio had never known. His brand of politics, which called for responsible party leadership which in turn demanded allegiance of the voters, was gone, with no sign that it would ever return.

De Sapio faced a jury of nine women and three men, picked after a total of forty prospects had been examined. The judge was Harold Tyler, a mild-mannered upstate New Yorker with no personal background in New York City politics. The trial lasted twenty-one days.

The record of the De Sapio trial is cluttered with hundreds of pages of examination and cross-examination of witnesses who attended the Germantown lawn party, testifying as to who met whom and who ate what. There was even a post-trial, pre-sentencing flurry when the defense produced witnesses who changed details of the stories given previously and argued that the jury had probably been influenced by earlier conflicts in the stories told by innocent bystanders. But there was no successful challenge to Itkin's story that he went there to meet De Sapio, at Fried's suggestion.

Thereafter, according to Itkin, he renewed the acquaintanceship with De Sapio in New York City and made at least three visits to the De Sapio apartment at 11 Fifth Avenue. He described in detail the private entrance to the den used by De Sapio for business conferences, and testified that on each of these visits De Sapio gave him money, emanating from Fried. The money, he said, was to be shared by Itkin, Marcus, and Corallo, in return for Marcus's exerting pressure on Con Edison to get construction contracts for Fried. The money handed him totaled $12,500, he swore, and he produced the original wrappers in which the money had been packed by a Long Island bank.

Itkin was not the only witness against De Sapio and Corallo, who was tried and convicted with De Sapio. Another was Marcus, who had already finished serving eighteen months for accepting the kickback on the reservoir contract and was given immunity in exchange for testifying against De Sapio in the Con Edison case.

The weapon Marcus said he used to swing contracts to Fried was a permit Con Edison needed to reconstruct a power line crossing city watershed and reservoir properties in Putnam County so that the line could carry higher voltages. The company ran into nothing but delays in the Department of Water Supply, and Charles Luce, the company's new top executive, had gone directly to Mayor Lindsay to see what could be done. But Lindsay had referred him back to Marcus, who had explained to the mayor that additional time was needed to make sure the city got proper fees from Con Edison for the expansion of its privilege.

Marcus, conceding he had never met or talked with De Sapio, said he got De Sapio's instructions on how to deal with Con Edison through Itkin. Itkin told him, Marcus said, not to meet with or discuss the permit with the Con Edison people until De Sapio informed Itkin the time was ripe.

Another prosecution witness was Gerald Hadden, a $50,000-a-year vice-president of the utility, who admitted he had received $15,000 in kickbacks from Fried and had stowed the money away in his safe-deposit box. (At an earlier stage of the investigation he staggered Hogan and his staff by dramatically producing the packets of bills in the grand-jury room.) Hadden testified that he and another Con Edison official, having lunch in a posh East Side restaurant, had been joined by De Sapio and that when the question of Con Edison's difficulties in getting permits from the city arose, De Sapio offered himself as a go-between, saying, "I'll see what I can do."

Hadden quoted himself as having said: "No one is entitled to any money," and De Sapio as having answered: "Maybe there should be a token of good faith."

Still a third witness was W. Dunham Crawford, another Con Edison official, who testified that Henry Fried had told him, "There is going to be a full exposé, De Sapio has been subpoenaed." When Crawford asked why Con Edison should get excited about the matter, Fried replied, "Hadden is a party to it."

A final witness of importance was a twenty-three-year-old former secretary of Itkin's, who testified that several times during the last four months of 1967 she had received in Itkin's office telephone calls from a woman who said that Mr. De Sapio was on the line and wished to speak to Mr. Itkin, and that she had put the calls through to her boss. Her testimony bolstered Itkin's contention that he had been in frequent touch with De Sapio, a circumstance which De Sapio firmly and consistently denied.

In the original interviews in Hogan's office, De Sapio had taken the position that he knew Itkin casually, as he did so many people. He did not recall meeting him at Fried's farm, and his first real recollection was when Itkin sought him out in the lobby of the Hotel Biltmore, recalled a previous acquaintanceship, talked politics, and sought De Sapio's advice on family problems. De Sapio denied any involvement with either Itkin or Marcus on Con Edison permits or Fried contracts. He stuck staunchly to that position in his trial, and the prosecution made the most of the conflict between his testimony and that of Itkin and Hadden.

When the trial was over, lawyers connected with the prosecution told the author they felt De Sapio's defense had made a serious tactical error in not disowning those original denials. They suggested that De Sapio, after hearing the whole case against him, could have turned to the jury and said, in effect, "Yes, I was involved to the extent of trying to do a favor for some friends. I denied it originally to keep them out of trouble, but I did intercede to get permits for Con Edison and some construction contracts for Fried. But I did not take any money and I did not pass any money to Itkin to bribe Marcus."

If he had taken that tack, they suggested, the case against him would have boiled down to the issue of Itkin's word against his, with no supporting testimony any longer worthy of consideration. The case went to the jury on December 12, just two days after De Sapio's sixty-first birthday. The jury was locked up for the night without having agreed on a verdict, but returned its decision—guilty—at noon the following day.

De Sapio's only comment to the press, as he stood erect and dignified amid the courtroom hubbub, was "It won't be a Merry Christmas."

The prosecution asked Judge Tyler to fix bail for De Sapio to make sure that he would be available for sentencing. The judge refused to require that kind of guarantee, saying, "Mr. De Sapio is part of New York City. I don't think he can fail to be around. This is his city."

On the day set for sentencing, February 10, 1970, De Sapio was there, with attorney Edelbaum and prosecutor Paul Rooney, each to have his final say before Judge Tyler made his ruling.

Rooney's plea was the expected one for a substantial jail term. He said: "I think this case is important . . . because too many people have lost faith in our legal system. The poor, the blacks, the man in the street, many of them are skeptical and feel we never go after, much less convict, the big-timers, the money men. What Carmine De Sapio did was to abuse public trust, not that given to those elected to public office, but a trust given to a community leader who used his reputation as a shield behind which to hide."

To aid Judge Tyler to decide what kind of man he had before him and to impose therefore an appropriate sentence, there was the usual pre-sentence report prepared by a probation officer. Judge Tyler had shown it to Edelbaum, who used it to bolster an impassioned plea for leniency:

I don't think in all my 42 years at the bar that I have ever read a better testimonial about the life of a man who has lived on this earth for 61 years, the perfect husband, the perfect father, the perfect son.

Tammany Hall politician? Nothing like that. He created a new image in the City of New York when he became leader and literally clawed his way to the top. He was responsible for some of the most fantastic reforms in political circles in the City of New York. The probation report shows he was responsible for fine judicial candidates; he was responsible for the first black man to become a judge; he was responsible for the first woman to become a judge. Everything he did as a politician was to change the image of Tammany Hall.

I have walked around the city since I was retained in this trial. I have met hundreds of people from all walks of life, both before and after the verdict; high people, low people, people of modest circumstances, elevator operators, cleaning women, high people, high judges, and all I have heard about Carmine De Sapio is that he is a fine and wonderful man.

If it should turn out some day, somehow, that this [verdict] is a terrible mistake, wouldn't it be horrendous to send such an individual to jail, with his background and what he has done in his lifetime?

Judge Tyler, fully aware that the probation report was in this case based primarily on interviews with De Sapio's family and friends, disagreed with Edelbaum on its significance:

I agree with you that this pre-sentence report reflects nothing but good about your client, Mr. Edelbaum. It is in many ways the most astonishing document I ever read.

I would be remiss and lacking in candor, however, if I failed to point out that probably the writer thereof was not present, as I was, in our trial. He did not know or hear the things I heard. I have already observed that the proof in this case was overwhelming, at least in the sense that there was overwhelming proof from which the jury as trier of the facts could reach the verdict that it did.

Half turning to the defendant, he continued:

I am sorry to say that this trial evidence presents a different side, which I think as a judge of this court I must bear in mind when I impose sentence. I cannot ignore the good work and the good parts of Carmine De Sapio; they have been demonstrated and they are part of the public record and need not be repeated by me or any probation officer. I think the public, particularly the public in your home community, Mr. De Sapio, justly like you and respect you for the things you have done for your church as well as things you have done for other community organizations.

But I regard this offense as catastrophic and of shattering significance in the affairs of our city. I do not think there can be anything regarded as more serious, and I have made my determination based upon what I heard at the trial in large part, hoping as God be my judge, that I also recognize the good work which is amply cited here, which we know in any event, and which I cannot ignore, of course.

In imposing a sentence of two years in jail and a fine of $4,500 —both stayed pending appeal—Judge Tyler told De Sapio: "There is no prison that I ever heard of that is necessary to rehabilitate you in the classic and precise sense of that term. . . . The only possible theoretical, and practical, and legal underpinning of any sentence that this or any other court can impose on you would have to be pinned on what we call deterrence."

The word "deterrence" in its legal famework, referred not to deterring De Sapio from committing the same crime again, but to deterring others in government and politics.

The judge then added: "I might have imposed a greater sentence had it not been for your age, the good works you have done, and my own sadness to see a man, who for all I know—though I never met you to my knowledge before this trial began—is a very likeable man."

De Sapio's last words to the court were delivered before Judge Tyler's final declaration of sentence, but after the judge's evaluation of the crime. He spoke quietly as he made his final protestation of innocence:

I do not disagree as to the catastrophic attitudes that reflect themselves in a matter of this kind. I think perhaps maybe outside of yourself, Your Honor, I have had sufficient or more experience in the area of sensitivity of public trust and the violation thereof; and I know that is perhaps the key factor, as Mr. Rooney sought to outline. Notwithstanding whatever I have done in the past, I should not be made an exception. I am very much aware of this, Your Honor.

There is only one thing that is rather difficult for me to absorb—and I appreciate and am aware of Your Honor's comments relative to the evidence supposedly being overwhelming at the trial—but I can only tell you about myself, notwithstanding the jury's verdict.

I took the witness stand. I tried to prepare a defense for myself. I tried to prove I was innocent. I was telling the truth. I am not casting any dishonorable reflections on other witnesses in terms of their credibility, although I am certain as we are all in this room, there were some and perhaps many who in order to cast reflection from themselves were motivated in saying or doing whatever they said or did, and I don't want to go into specifics . . . but I just don't understand, Your Honor, why I am a defendant, or as I have been, why there have not been many other defendants . . .

This is a tragic day for me and my wife and my daughter and my father, and many sincere and loyal friends who professed a degree of confidence in me over a period of years who I feel this particular time have been let down by my stigmatism, or pollution, to use Mr. Rooney's word.

I think and hope some day the truth will out. I haven't sought to, I haven't designed and I never meant, now in this trial or any time in the history of my time in public affairs, to engage in any corrupt activities and there is a record of that. Perhaps I have been the victim of an aura, a climate that is concerning many people relative to organized crime.

All I want to say to you is that I never had anything to do with organized crime and never would have anything to do with it, notwithstanding all the temptations, all the machinations and all the problems that concern themselves—as you aptly put it one day in the robing room—with big cities. I have done everything to the best of my ability to maintain—preserve the kind of reputation I think I earned for my family and friends. I am sorry it has turned out this way, and I just hope, Your Honor, that some day in the future it [the truth] will be brought to light.

Thank you very kindly.

On November 16, 1970, the United States Court of Appeals upheld the De Sapio conviction. Judge Henry J. Friendly, writing for himself and his colleagues, J. Joseph Smith and Paul R. Hays, found that De Sapio "was accorded a fair trial conforming to law."

The Supreme Court of the United States declined to review, and on June 25, 1971, he was driven by friends to the doors of the Federal Penitentiary at Lewisburg, Pennsylvania, and entered as an inmate.

INDEX

225